connexions

Penguin Education

a series of topic books for students in school and colleges of further education

Colin Ward

WORK

General Editor
Richard Mabey

Art Editor
Arthur Lockwood

Penguin Education
Penguin Books Ltd,
Harmondsworth, Middlesex, England
Penguin Books Inc,
7110 Ambassador Road,
Baltimore, Md 21207, U.S.A.
Penguin Books Australia Ltd,
Ringwood, Victoria, Australia
Penguin Books Canada Ltd,
41 Steelcase Road West,
Markham, Ontario, Canada
Penguin Books (N.Z.) Ltd,
182-190 Wairau Road,
Auckland 10, New Zealand

First published 1972
Reprinted 1974, 1975

Made and printed in Great Britain by
Compton Printing Ltd, Aylesbury
Set in Monophoto Century and Univers

Got up at six o'clock, after being called about five times by my elder brother, got washed and dressed, had a cup of tea and went to work. When I got to work I got my delivery sheets – there were nine pubs to do over Enfield way, and I went with my usual driver. We had to load up the lorry first of all and then unload when we got to the different pubs. We also have to pick up their empties, which is all commission to us – we get paid threepence on a barrel; this may not sound a lot but you earn quite a bit. My basic wage is £11 9s., but I earn between £15 and £21 a week, and you don't sneer at that. One of the pubs we went to had got cellars older than anyone can remember. It still has the old wine vaults; the public house has been rebuilt, but the cellar has been unchanged. It's now very musty and the floors are slippery as the damp forms slime on the old flat-stones, so it's still a good place to keep beer in – it stays cool all the time. With one of the pubs we went to the publican seemed rather moany. With people like that you have to be ready to give quick answers to all their complaints. It gets maddening at times, as if you say the wrong thing they phone the Transport Office about you. The only way you can get back is say you will report them for dirty cellars. Some of the stillons are disgusting – a stillon is what we have to place the beer on, and if they're not clean the keg slides and could easily trap your fingers. We got back to the depot at about 3.45 and as the day was hot the free beer at the depot was very welcome. It's not as strong as the beer at a pub, but when you're thirsty it tastes all right. After that I went home.

An eighteen-year-old brewery dray boy describes a day's work

It's the mixture for most people today: a bit of bickering, a lot of drudgery, the ghost of some kind of skill.

It's WORK – the four-letter life sentence.

SO WHY DO WE DO IT?

One answer is that every human community is a network of people, each of them making his own contribution: the farmer feeding them all, the builder housing them all, the tailor clothing them all – the fairytale picture of the division of labour in society. But what proportion of jobs are actually like this?

Another answer is that work, whatever it is, is just the way in which we buy spending power, the way we earn our leisure: 'Each day, men sell little pieces of themselves in order to try to buy them back each night and weekend with the coin of fun.'

Another answer is that work is what gives human beings their self-respect and the respect of others, and is the deepest source of achievement and satisfaction in life. 'I believe in the dignity of labour,' said a character in one of Bernard Shaw's plays. 'That's because you've never done any,' came the reply.

Yet another answer is that while work was a necessity in the bad old days, it is just a bad habit we have got to get over in the coming age of leisure, just a hangover from the days before automation, and that people who don't work are the fore-runners of the full-time fun future.

Perhaps all the answers are true for some people and some jobs. Are they true for you? Are there any other answers? These are the questions this book asks.

There are two basic kinds of animals: the specialists and the opportunists. The specialists are those which have evolved one supreme survival device on which they depend for their very existence, and which dominates their lives. Such creatures are the ant-eaters, the koalas, the giant pandas, the snakes and the eagles. So long as ant-eaters have their ants, koalas have their eucalyptus leaves, pandas have their bamboo shoots, and snakes and eagles have their prey, they can relax.

The opportunists are not so fortunate. They are the species – such as dogs and wolves, racoons and coatis, and monkeys and apes – that have evolved no single specialized survival device. They are jacks of all trades, always on the look-out for any small advantage the environment has to offer. In the wild, they never stop exploring and investigating. Anything and everything is examined in case it may add yet another string to the bow of survival. They cannot afford to relax for very long and evolution has made sure that they do not. They have evolved nervous systems that abhor inactivity, that keep them constantly on the go. Of all species, it is man himself who is the supreme opportunist. Like the others, he is intensely exploratory. Like them, he has a biologically built-in demand for a high stimulus input from his environment. Our early tribal ancestor did not find this such a difficult problem. The demands of survival kept him busy. It required all his time and energy to stay alive, to find food and water, to defend his territory, to avoid his enemies, to breed and rear his young and to construct and maintain his shelter.

from *The Human Zoo* by Desmond Morris

Ant or man, the job looks the same. Ants have always had a reputation for being highly industrious creatures. Yet a top American biologist recently found that 'individual ants spend a great deal of time just loafing'. So who's to say that it isn't 'natural' to be lazy?

Is it natural?

Is it *natural* for men to work? Or, for that matter, is it *natural* for us to be lazy? We don't know, because there is really no such thing as a natural man, nor such a thing as human nature. We are all the result, not only of our genetic inheritance from our parents, but also of the ready-made surroundings in which we grew up, and of the way they brought us up. If you isolated a baby from other people so that it had no human contacts, it would not become a 'person' at all.

We can see this from the cases that have occasionally been found of *feral* or wolf-children. People thought that the wild child found in the woods or the jungle had been lost or stolen as a baby and reared by wolves, and that this explained its wolf-like behaviour. (The idea appears all through history, from Romulus and Remus, the legendary twins who founded Rome, to *The Jungle Book*.)

In 1731 a 'wild girl' was found in a wood near Châlons-sur-Marne in France. 'She possessed a monkey-like agility which enabled her to catch birds and rabbits; these she skinned with her nails and gobbled raw, as would a dog. She delighted to suck the blood from living pigeons, and had no speech except hideous screams and howls.' And in 1798 an old lady gathering mushrooms in the woods at Caune was frightened by a strange animal. The whole village turned out with dogs and caught what turned out to be a boy of about eleven, naked, mute, walking almost on all fours; a Paris doctor, Jean Itard, spent five years trying to train him into humanity. And about fifty years ago in the Indian province of Orissa, two wolf girls were discovered. One of them, Kamala, was about eight years old, and after years of training – to walk on two legs, to use plates and spoons, and to put two words together – she died, imprisoned in babyhood still, at eighteen. Modern scientists do not believe that these unhappy children were reared by animals: they think that they were grossly neglected and abandoned by their relations: 'There are no wolf-children, only wolf-parents.'

But ordinary humans – and most animals – are reared by an older generation. In the most primitive societies parents teach their children to hunt food and make shelter. And in every society the play of children is an imitation of the work of adults: a kind of rehearsal of the real thing.

Certainly *activity* – whether work or play – seems to be a necessity of life. When we say we are doing *nothing*, we mean that we are doing nothing with a purpose. A healthy human being cannot stand being prevented from doing *anything*. Psychologists tried experiments with volunteers who were isolated in small cubicles wearing opaque goggles and heavy gloves that prevented small hand actions. It was found that the volunteers desperately chose any activity to break the monotony – they whistled, talked to themselves, tapped out rhythms, but soon showed signs of such severe stress that the experiments had to be called off. Intense boredom was driving them mad.

Boredom of the ordinary mild kind can kill too. We can all think of examples of the man who, after fifty years' service with the old firm, gets his gold watch and retires at sixty-five. A few months later, his colleagues, who had a whip-round to buy him a new telly as a retirement present, are making a collection again – for a wreath. No, he didn't die of anything in particular. He just pottered around for a while. Of course he didn't actually have any hobbies. After a while he stopped going out. His wife took him breakfast in bed. Bored to death really.

This Eskimo is learning whilst he plays. He has to – if he is to survive. In a few years the bow he is holding will be a full-sized, lethal, hunting weapon.

1 STARTING WORK

Child's play

Children's play is modelled on the work of the adult world. We think it natural for small children to play at being grown up, and yet (writes Joe Benjamin) as soon as a child is old enough to see through the pretence and demand the reality we 'try to fob him off with games and activities which seem only to put off the day when he will enter the world proper'.

At one time children could 'help' the blacksmith, the builder or the wheelwright, but the modern town child may often have no idea what his father does at work, miles away from home. Dad goes off in the morning and comes back in the evening, but his children may never see the inside of the factory or office until they actually start work themselves.

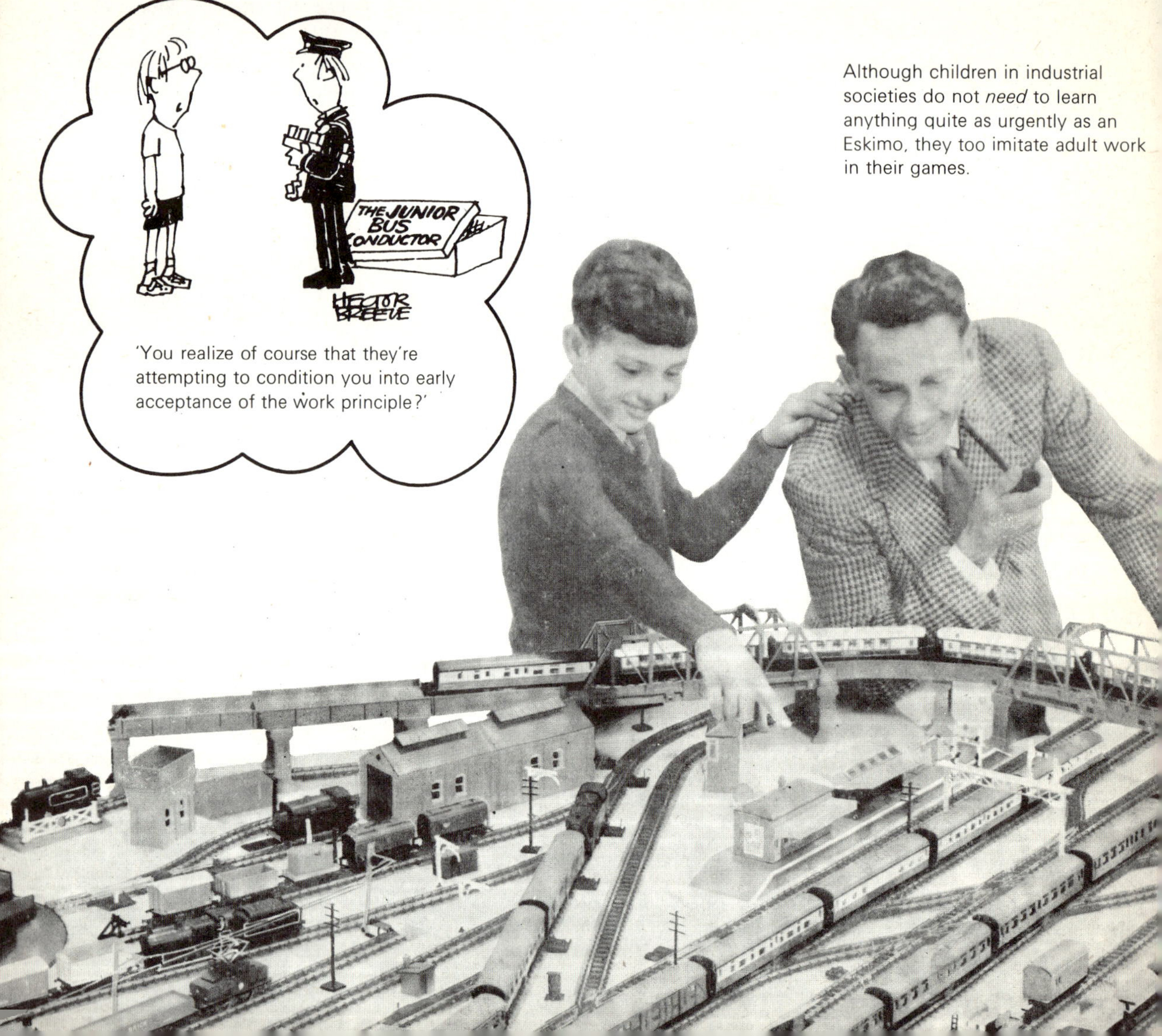

'You realize of course that they're attempting to condition you into early acceptance of the work principle?'

Although children in industrial societies do not *need* to learn anything quite as urgently as an Eskimo, they too imitate adult work in their games.

I STILL HAVEN'T FOUND A REALLY SURE-FIRE DODGE TO MAKE ME SOME MONEY.

Working children

The law today shuts children out of the world of work, and, knowing about the ruthless exploitation of children as factory slaves in the nineteenth century, we can be thankful for this. Yet is it altogether a good thing in modern conditions? No boy or girl with a paper-round or a holiday job would think so.

But do you think in the same way about this kind of pocket-money job as about the work you are going to do day-in, day-out for a lifetime? Should you?

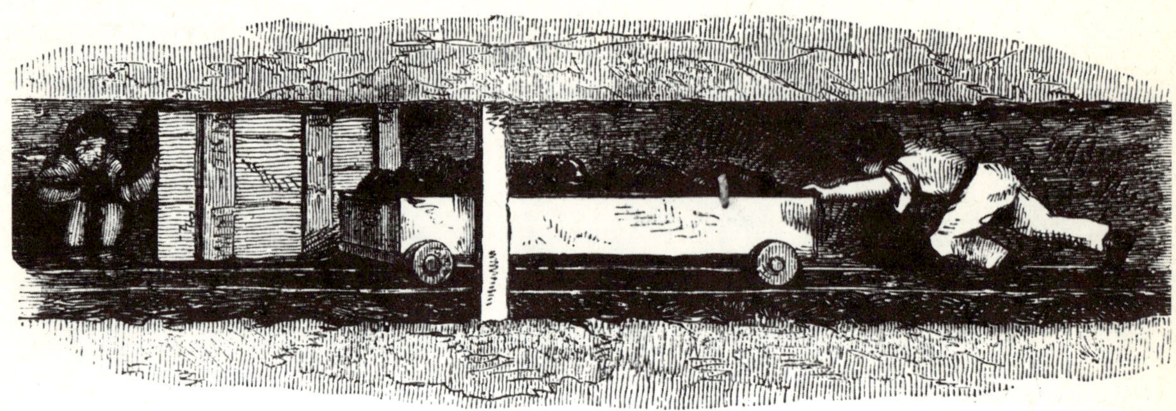

Young miners in England, 1820s.

Young miners in America, 1911.

13-year-olds could lose paper rounds

by Anna Sproule

The Home Office is to ask teachers, local authorities, employers' organizations, and the Trades Union Congress whether children between 13 and 14 years old should be allowed to do newspaper rounds and other part-time work after 1972.

When the school leaving age is raised in that year, the minimum age for employment will automatically go up to 14 unless the law is changed, and the Government thinks that this is a good time to review the whole question.

A special memorandum released by the Home Office this week points out that the youngest age at which a child can do part-time work out of school is 13 in most areas of the country. Forty-one local education authorities, however, have already raised this limit by one year, thus anticipating the raising of school leaving age on their own account.

A major effect of the raising of the leaving age will be to bring a completely new age-range of children—those between 15 and 16—under the ban on full-time work. This is one of the points that the Home Office wants discussed by teachers and other organizations.

"It may be argued on the one hand," says the memorandum, "that the beneficial effects of the raising of the school leaving age will be nullified if 15-year-old pupils are to be free to tire themselves out in gainful employment at weekends, during holidays and part-time on school days.

"On the other hand, given the earlier maturing of young people now, it may seem difficult to argue that a 15-year-old in 1972-73 and thereafter ought not to be allowed to undertake the kind of work which a 15-year-old in 1970 is permitted to do; always provided that his work is not such as to interfere directly with his education, and is for the most part confined to weekends and holidays."

The Home Office particularly wants to know whether hours of work and the "prohibited employments" list should be the same throughout the 13-16 age range, or whether they should vary with age. Prohibited employments at the moment include work in a barber's shop, in restaurant kitchens, and in "places of public entertainment".

Progress can be double-edged. These children have just been sacked from a factory where they were employed during their school holidays for 10p an hour. The reason? The employer was accused by parents and others of going back to 'child slave-labour' of the sort illustrated on the facing page. But the children themselves enjoyed the work (sticking labels on bottles). Said one: 'I just wanted to earn enough to buy myself some new clothes.'

Choosing a job for Billy Casper

'Now then, Casper, what kind of job had you in mind?'

He shunted the record cards to one side, and replaced them with a blank form, lined and sectioned for the relevant information. CASPER, WILLIAM, in red on the top line. He copied age, address and other details from the record card, then changed pens and looked up.

'Well?'

'I don't know, I haven't thought about it right.'

'Well you should be thinking about it. You want to start off on the right foot, don't you?'

'I suppose so.'

'You haven't looked round for anything yet then?'

'No, not yet.'

'Well what would you like to do? What are you good at?'

He consulted Billy's record card again.

'Offices held. . . . Aptitudes and Abilities . . . right then . . . would you like to work in an office? Or would you prefer manual work?'

'What's that, manual work?'

'It means working with your hands, for example, building, farming, engineering, jobs like that, as opposed to pen-pushing jobs.'

'I'd be all right working in an office, wouldn't I? I've a job to read and write.'

The Employment Officer printed MANUAL on the form, then raised his pen hand as though he was going to print it again on the top of his head. He scratched it instead, and the nails left white scratches on the skin. He smoothed his fingers carefully across the plot of hair, then looked up. Billy was staring straight past him out of the window.

'Have you thought about entering a trade as an apprentice? You know, as an electrician, or a bricklayer or something like that. Of course the money isn't too good while you're serving your apprenticeship. You may find that lads of your own age who take dead-end jobs will be earning far more than you; but in those jobs there's no satisfaction or security, and if you do stick it out you'll find it well worth your while. And whatever happens, at least you'll always have a trade at your finger tips won't you?

'Well, what do you think about it? And as you've already said you feel better working with your hands, perhaps this would be your best bet. Of course this would mean attending Technical College and studying for various examinations, but nowadays most employers encourage their lads to take advantage of these facilities, and allow them time off to attend, usually one day a week. On the other hand, if your firm wouldn't allow you time off in the day, and you were still keen to study, then you'd have to attend classes in your own time. Some lads do it. Some do it for years, two and three nights a week from leaving school, right up to their middle twenties, when some of them take their Higher National, and even degrees.

'But you've got to if you want to get on in life. And they'll all tell you that it's worth it in the end. . . . Had you considered continuing your education in any form after leaving? . . . I say, are you listening, lad?'

'Yes.'

'You don't look as though you are to me. I haven't got all day you know, I've other lads to see before four o'clock.'

He looked down at Billy's form again.

'Now then, where were we? Oh, yes. Well if nothing I've mentioned already appeals to you, and if you can stand a hard day's graft, and you don't mind getting dirty, then there are good opportunities in mining. . . .'

'I'm not goin' down t'pit.'

'Conditions have improved tremendously. . . .'

'I wouldn't be seen dead down t'pit.'

'Well what do you want to do then? There doesn't seem to be a job in England to suit you.'

He scrutinized Billy's record card again as though there might be a hint of one there.

'What about hobbies? What hobbies have you got? Do you like gardening, or constructing Meccano sets, or anything like that?'

Billy shook his head slowly.

'Don't you have any hobbies at all?'

Billy looked at him for a moment, then stood up quickly.

'Can I go now?'

from *A Kestrel for a Knave* by Barry Hines

Answer to quiz opposite:

On the average, people tend to place them in the order in which they are printed here. Does this surprise you?

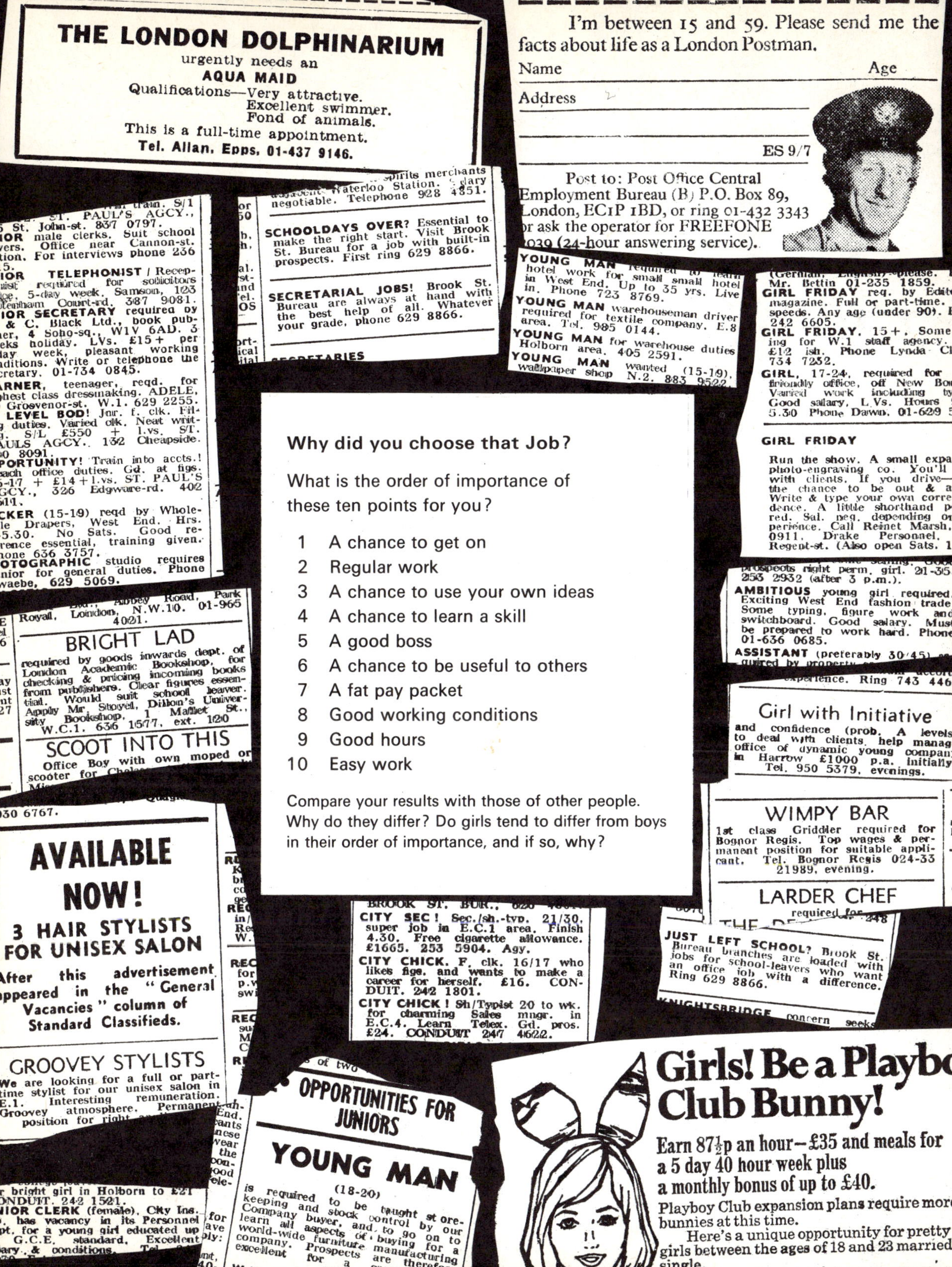

Why did you choose that Job?

What is the order of importance of these ten points for you?

1. A chance to get on
2. Regular work
3. A chance to use your own ideas
4. A chance to learn a skill
5. A good boss
6. A chance to be useful to others
7. A fat pay packet
8. Good working conditions
9. Good hours
10. Easy work

Compare your results with those of other people. Why do they differ? Do girls tend to differ from boys in their order of importance, and if so, why?

The initiation

The cast

Spow	a fitter and turner
Boswell	an apprentice fitter
Garret	a fitter and turner
Bagley	an apprentice welder
Betty	a machine minder
Linda	a machine minder
Taffy	a doorkeeper
Dicker	an apprentice fitter
Harry	an apprentice fitter
Wags	an apprentice fitter
Jimmy	an apprentice sheet-metal worker
Jeff	an apprentice fitter
Mr Bradbury	a foreman

[SPOW *and* GARRET. *Enter new* APPRENTICE.]

SPOW: You a new apprentice then, son?

BOSWELL: Yes. I've just started.

SPOW: Has your Mum ironed your overalls?

GARRET: Funny time of year to start.

BOSWELL: I had tried to stay at school, then left. I'm a special case.

SPOW: We're all bloody special cases here, son. Aren't we, Garret? Special cases.

GARRET: You'll be a special case afore long.

SPOW: You must be a special case to come here. There's lots of openings in the world without locking yourself in behind those prison walls.

BOSWELL: You're in.

SPOW: In our days things were worse.

GARRET: You had to be grateful for what you got.

SPOW: You were glad to get in anywhere.

GARRET: There were queues to be an apprentice in them days.

SPOW: And if you could get on the Railway . . .

GARRET: Or police . . .

SPOW: Or owt pensionable like that, why you thought you were in luxury.

GARRET: But now, you get it all for nowt.

[*Enter* BAGLEY *and* APPRENTICES.]

BAGLEY: When we get a new apprentice . . .

ALL: We introduce him to the trade,
Down with his trousers,
See if he can make the grade.

[*They initiate him.*]

VOICES: In, grease him up. Harder than that man, let's hear him. Come on, grease his nipple.

BETTY and LINDA: Leave him alone. Leave him be. Can you not see he's had enough, leave him be.

VOICES: Keep bloody out of it. Keep bloody out of it. Once girls were done.

BETTY and LINDA: Leave him be. Leave him be.

[*They stand back.*]

BETTY: Now look what you've done, he's crying.

LINDA: Let him get up.

BAGLEY: Why, it was nothing.

BETTY: Look what you've done. You big stiff. It's all right for you, you bloody bull, you can take it.

BAGLEY: You can take it, can't you kid?

SPOW: Are you O.K., son? He's got spectacles on.

BAGLEY: Why didn't somebody say he had spectacles on? Are they bust, son?

BOSWELL: No. I thought they were. They're not.

BAGLEY: Are you all right then? Course you are, aren't you, son? All right? You must be all right. You're just crying for your specs, son, aren't you?

BOSWELL: Yes.

BAGLEY: He's just crying about his specs, you see. He thought they were broken. Why, he took it well, didn't you, kid? You've got to take it. He took it.

TAFFY: I don't know what you want to be doing that for. It's bloody dangerous, not to say vulgar.

DICKER: He's a Welsh Puritan.

TAFFY: I'm against it, man. It's like *Tom Brown's Schooldays*.

BAGLEY: It's a tradition. Like Welsh Rarebit.

TAFFY: Traditions in Wales are beautiful. Not vulgar like this.

HARRY: Wales is beautiful. I've been there camping, mountains and lakes.

TAFFY: I don't like your English traditions, your flaming Morris Dancers and rugby players hanging knickers on goal-posts.

BAGLEY: What about Welsh rugby players and their leeks?

TAFFY: The leek is a more manly symbol than a pair of knickers. And as for this habit, this initiation, I think it's barbaric.

BAGLEY: It isn't barbaric. I had it.

WAGS: What does that prove? I think Taffy is right. Do away with it.

JIMMY: Keep it in. I like it.

TAFFY: There we are, that split personality likes it. You better do away with it.

JEFF: I think it would be best done away with.

BAGLEY: The moulders make a mould of their apprentices, don't they? And the pattern makers nail them to a pattern; we'll have nothing left.

HARRY: It'll hit the tourist industry.

TAFFY: Well, I say do away with it. Just take an apprentice in. Do something symbolic if you like. Like crossing the equator on a ship.

GARRET: We did that on the troopships, that's good fun. With old Father Neptune.

BAGLEY: Old Father Neptune? He would die for want of sea water up here.

HARRY: He could come by canal.

BETTY: I think it should be done away with. Especially with girls around.

SPOW: Girls used to do it worse than the men once upon a time.

GARRET: Do you remember what they used to do in the Rope Works?

JIMMY: What did they do in the Rope Works?

GARRET: Has the boxing knocked your imagination out of you?

SPOW: And the ropes were all gauges.

BETTY: This isn't the Rope Works.

LINDA: And that was before the war.

TAFFY: Do away with it. If I can get you to do away with it then my departure from Wales will not have been in vain.

BAGLEY: Look, the kid doesn't mind. Do you, kid?

BOSWELL: No. I don't mind.

JEFF: Now it's over. Nobody minds once it's over. They want to see somebody else receive it.

JIMMY: Don't spoil the sport. Keep it on.

BAGLEY: We'll take a vote on it. I'll make the closing speech. Gentlemen, lads, fellow lads, any others; womenfolk; I support the retention of initiation because it makes us all a band of brothers, happy brothers, we few, standing at our machines. Other societies have it, the Freemasons, the Buffaloes, the Order of the Garter –

TAFFY: If you think, to get the Order of the Garter, you get your testicles plastered then you must be mad.

SPOW: It would have ruined Montgomery at his age.

JEFF: I'm with Taffy, I'm against the Initiation. I think it's humiliating. I think it's just kept on to give the *old men* a thrill.

SPOW: Who are you looking at, you cheeky lump.

BETTY: I'm against it. This is a mixed yard.

LINDA: We don't like your nasty habits.

Is one of the purposes of these initiation rites to provide the older workers with a chance to get the boredom and frustration out of their systems; to say, in effect, 'It's been rough for us, and we're damned if it's going to be easier for you'? In the film *Metropolis* (*below*) the workers take it out on the machine instead.

BAGLEY: What does Mabel think?

HARRY: It's her only form of enjoyment.

BETTY: Leave Mabel out of it. That's the trouble with you, Bagley. You always turn on the quiet ones. You don't know what it's like to be hurt. You've got no feelings.

BAGLEY: I've got feelings. I wept buckets when City lost the Cup.

JEFF: Let's have a vote on it then. Who is in favour of the abolition of the Initiation? All in favour say Aye.

[*Not many.*]

BAGLEY: Now, vote for retention. And never mind this mumbling in your shirt collars. I want to see hands up. See who's voting.

JEFF: That's intimidation.

BAGLEY: It isn't. I just want to know who my friends are. Hands up, if you wish to retain the traditions of the factory, the historical usages of the firm, the long line of continued development of the yard. . . .

JEFF: If Mr Raines could hear you now, there'd be a rush to the Stock Exchange to buy shares.

BAGLEY: Hands aloft.

[*Hands go up. Enter* MR BRADBURY.]

MR BRADBURY: Bagley! what's this? A strike meeting?

BAGLEY: Yes, Mr Bradbury, we're all walking out. Exodus. I'm Moses. We're off to Freedom, Mr Bradbury. Tell Mr Raines, the machines will have to mind themselves.

MR BRADBURY: What is it now, lads? You've got nothing to complain about. We don't want trouble here, this isn't the Motor Works . . . you've got a Welfare Officer.

BAGLEY: Stop worrying! Right lads, motion unanimously carried.

[*The crowd disperses.*]

from *The Apprentices* by Peter Terson

Apprenticeship is a very ancient system of training for work, and a lot of people think it quite out of date for modern industry. Why do we keep it? The answer is because it suits everybody. It suits parents who want their sons to learn a trade. It suits boys who want the pride and independence that go with earning a living – even if the earnings are low. It suits some employers because it provides cut-price labour. It suits the unions because it regulates entry into the trade. What alternatives can you think of that would be better?

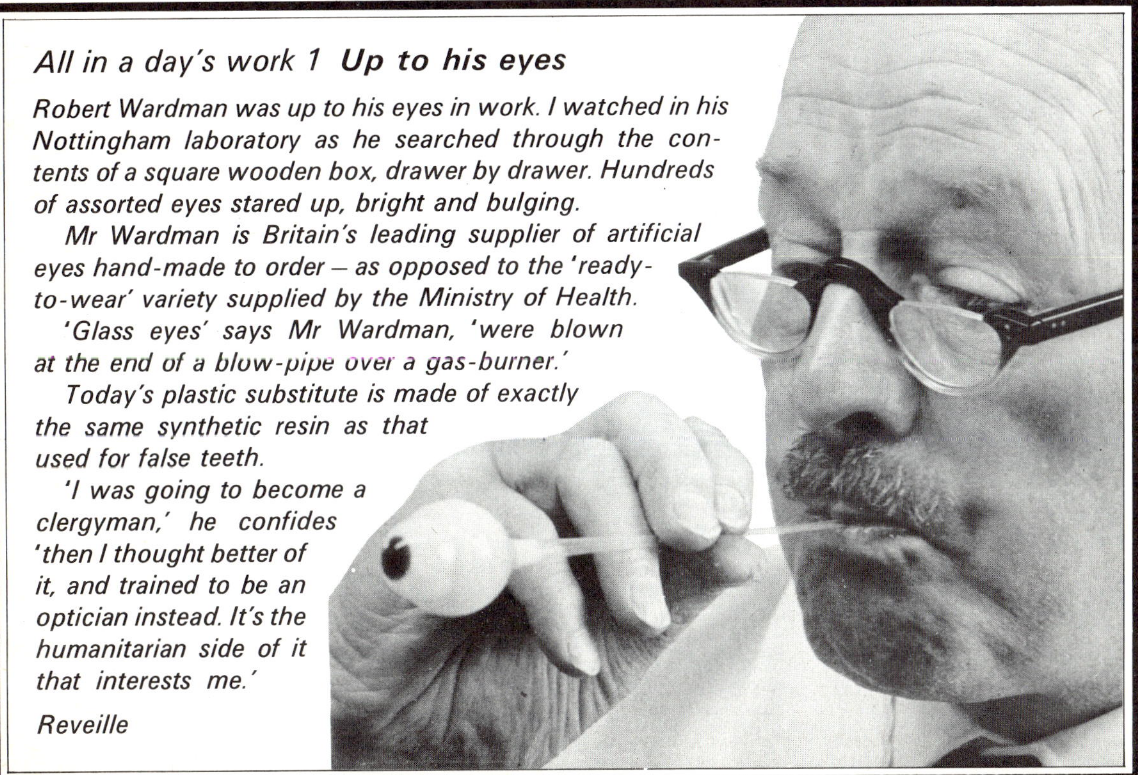

All in a day's work 1 ***Up to his eyes***

Robert Wardman was up to his eyes in work. I watched in his Nottingham laboratory as he searched through the contents of a square wooden box, drawer by drawer. Hundreds of assorted eyes stared up, bright and bulging.

Mr Wardman is Britain's leading supplier of artificial eyes hand-made to order – as opposed to the 'ready-to-wear' variety supplied by the Ministry of Health.

'Glass eyes' says Mr Wardman, 'were blown at the end of a blow-pipe over a gas-burner.'

Today's plastic substitute is made of exactly the same synthetic resin as that used for false teeth.

'I was going to become a clergyman,' he confides 'then I thought better of it, and trained to be an optician instead. It's the humanitarian side of it that interests me.'

Reveille

2 THE REALITY OF WORK

The splendour of work

The house-builder at work in cities or anywhere,
The preparatory jointing, squaring, sawing, mortising,
The hoist-up of beams, the push of them in their places, laying them regular,
Setting the studs by their tenons in the mortises according as they were prepared,
The blows of mallets and hammers, the attitudes of the men, their curved limbs,
Bending, standing, astride the beams, driving in pins, holding on by posts and braces,
The hooked arm over the plate, the other arm wielding the axe,
The floor-men forcing the planks close to be nailed,
Their postures bringing their weapons downward on the bearers,
The echoes resounding through the vacant building;
The huge storehouse carried up in the city well under way,
The six framing-men, two in the middle and two at each end, carefully bearing on their shoulders a heavy stick for a cross-beam,
The crowded line of masons with trowels in their right hands rapidly laying the long side-wall, two hundred feet front to rear,
The flexible rise and fall of backs, the continual click of the trowel striking the bricks,
The bricks one after another each laid so workmanlike in its place, and set with a knock of the trowel-handle,
The piles of materials, the mortar on the mortar-boards, and the steady replenishing by the hod-men;
Spar-makers in the spar-yard, the swarming row of well-grown apprentices,
The swing of their axes on the square-hewed log shaping it toward the shape of a mast,
The brisk short crackle of the steel driven slantingly into the pine,
The butter-colored chips flying off in great flakes and slivers,
The limber motion of brawny young arms and hips in easy costumes.

from *Song of the Broad Axe* by Walt Whitman

Right:
'Iron and coal'
Newcastle
1861

Whatsoever · thy · hand · findeth · to · do · do · it · with · thy · Might:
In the NINETEENTH
CENTURY, the Northumbrians

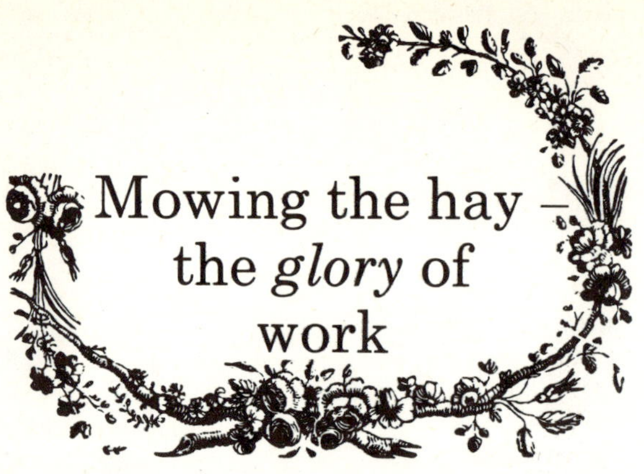

Mowing the hay – the *glory* of work

He thought of nothing, wished for nothing, except not to be left behind and to do his work as well as possible. He heard nothing save the swish of the knives, saw the receding upright figure of Titus in front of him, the crescent curve of the cut grass, the grass and flower-heads slowly and rhythmically falling about the blade of his scythe, and ahead of him the end of the row, where it would come to rest.

Suddenly, without understanding what it was or whence it came, in the midst of his toil, he felt a pleasant sensation of chill on his hot, perspiring shoulders. He glanced up at the sky while his scythe was being sharpened. A dark cloud was hanging low overhead and big drops of rain were falling. Some of the peasants went to put their coats on; others, like Levin, merely moved their shoulders up and down, enjoying the refreshing coolness.

Swath followed swath. They mowed long rows and short rows, good grass and poor grass. Levin lost all count of time and had no idea whether it was late or early. A change began to come over his work which gave him intense satisfaction. There were moments when he forgot what he was doing, he moved without effort and his line was almost as smooth and good as Titus's. But as soon as he began thinking what he was doing and trying to do better, he was at once conscious how hard the task was, and would mow badly. . . .

In the very heat of the day the mowing did not seem such hard work. The perspiration with which he was drenched cooled him, while the sun, that burned his back, his head, and his arms, bare to the elbow, gave a vigour and dogged energy to his labour; and more and more often now came these moments of oblivion, when it was possible not to think of what one was doing. The scythe cut of itself. Those were the happy moments. Still more delightful were the moments when they reached the river at the end of the rows and the old man would rub his scythe with a thick knot of wet grass, rinse the steel blade in the fresh water of the stream, ladle out a little in a tin dipper, and offer Levin a drink.

'What do you say to my home-brew, eh? Good eh?' he would say with a wink.

And truly Levin had never tasted any drink so good as this warm water with bits of grass floating in it and a rusty flavour from the tin dipper. And immediately after this came the blissful, slow saunter, with his hand on the scythe, during which he could wipe away the streaming sweat, fill his lungs with air, and look about at the long line of mowers and at what was happening around in the forest and the country.

The longer Levin mowed, the oftener he experienced those moments of oblivion when it was not his arms which swung the scythe but the scythe seemed to mow of itself, a body full of life and consciousness of its own, and as though by magic, without a thought being given to it, the work did itself regularly and carefully. These were the most blessed moments.

from *Anna Karenina* by Leo Tolstoy

The harvest – what price *glory*?

One of the technical means which the modern employer uses in order to secure the greatest possible amount of work from his men is the device of piece-rates. In agriculture, for instance, the gathering of the harvest is a case where the greatest possible intensity of labour is called for, since, the weather being uncertain, the difference between high profit and heavy loss may depend on the speed with which the harvesting can be done. Hence a system of piece-rates is almost universal in this case. And since the interest of the employer in a speeding-up of harvesting increases with the increase of the results and the intensity of the work, the attempt has again and again been made, by increasing the piece-rates of the workmen, thereby giving them an opportunity to earn what is for them a very high wage, to interest them in increasing their own efficiency. But a peculiar difficulty has been met with surprising frequency: raising the piece-rates has often had the result that not more but less has been accomplished in the same time, because the worker reacted to the increase not by increasing but by decreasing the amount of his work. A man, for instance, who at the rate of 1 mark per acre mowed two-and-a-half acres per day and earned $2\frac{1}{2}$ marks, when the rate was raised to 1·25 marks per acre, mowed, not three acres, as he might easily have done, thus earning 3·75 marks, but only two acres, so that he could still earn the $2\frac{1}{2}$ marks to which he was accustomed. The opportunity of earning more was less attractive than that of working less. He did not ask: how much can I earn in a day if I do as much work as possible? but: how much must I work in order to earn the wage, $2\frac{1}{2}$ marks, which I earned before and which takes care of my traditional needs? This is an example of what is here meant by traditionalism. A man does not 'by nature' wish to earn more and more money, but simply to live as he is accustomed to live and to earn as much as is necessary for that purpose. Wherever modern capitalism has begun its work of increasing the productivity of human labour by increasing its intensity, it has encountered the immensely stubborn resistance of this leading trait of pre-capitalistic labour.

from *The Protestant Ethic and the Spirit of Capitalism* by Max Weber

Where did the glory go?

For most people, most of the time, work hasn't been very glorious. All through history most people, even though they knew that work was a necessity of life, must have felt that the best thing about it was knocking off. But though our ancestors may have believed that a life of toil was God's punishment to Adam ('In the sweat of thy face shalt thou eat bread'), they also believed in having plenty of leisure. A craftsman's working day was shorter in the Middle Ages than it was in our grandparents' time, and the normal number of holidays (Holy Days) was about 115.

With the industrial revolution and the coming of the factory system, the number of days off was reduced until the law stepped in to establish public holidays on days when banks were shut, instead of days when the churches were open. Factory work demanded regular time-keeping and long hours.

The change in ideas about work is known by historians as the rise of the Protestant Ethic, because it, and the industrial system, came first in the countries where the Protestant form of Christianity had taken over from the traditional Catholic attitudes.

The Protestant Ethic

Remember that time is money. He that can earn ten shillings a day by his labour, and goes abroad, or sits idle, one half of that day, though he spends but sixpence during his diversion or idleness, ought not to reckon that the only expense; he has really spent, or rather thrown away five shillings besides.

Remember that credit is money. If a man lets his money lie in my hands after it is due, he gives me the interest, or so much as I can make of it during that time. This amounts to a considerable sum where a man has good and large credit, and makes good use of it.

Remember that money is of the prolific, generating nature. Money can beget money, and its offspring can beget more, and so on. Five shillings turned is six, turned again it is seven and threepence, and so on, till it becomes a hundred pounds. The more there is of it, the more it produces every turning, so that the profits rise quicker and quicker. He that kills a breeding-sow, destroys all her offspring to the thousandth generation. He that murders a crown, destroys all that it might have produced, even scores of pounds. . . .

The most trifling actions that affect a man's credit are to be regarded. The sound of your hammer at five in the morning, or eight at night, heard by a creditor, makes him easy six months longer; but if he sees you at a billiard-table, or hears your voice at a tavern, when you should be at work, he sends for his money the next day; demands it, before he can receive it, in a lump.

from *Advice to a Young Tradesman*
by Benjamin Franklin, 1748

End of the Protestant Ethic

The Protestant Ethic made a religion of work, but it is a religion which has lost many of its worshippers. Some jobs seem to us to be enjoyable in themselves, some give us companionship or status, but most jobs today are nothing more than an unavoidable chore to give us the cash to buy a living and some leisure.

An unemployed man, writing in the book *Work: Twenty Personal Accounts*, says,

Although there may be thousands of different kinds of jobs, as I see it there are basically only two kinds of work. One is the sort that in the main is done for its own sake. Attached to it are no notions of bosses or clocks or profits or wages and usually it proves rewarding in itself. The other sort is that which is normally done in return for a weekly wage at docks, in factories, on building sites, down pits where one is a slave to timekeeping, norms, incentives, procedures, to say nothing of a whole clutch of rubbishy intangibles such as getting ahead and status and all the rest of the carrot spiel with which we have been well and truly brainwashed.

Some of the people who described their jobs in this book find work enjoyable in itself. A research scientist finds his income 'quite a lot for doing what I would do anyway, even if I were rich' and he finds his fellow-workers 'cheerful, well-balanced people, since they too are doing what they like'. Some, like the railway signalwoman, grumble at times:

Who doesn't? How often have I cursed the job to all eternity on arriving at my cabin on a bitterly cold Monday morning to find everything frozen solid. Levers that seem to burn your hands when you touch them, they are so cold; points full of snow so that even an Amazon couldn't move the levers; signals pulled off on a Saturday night now frozen in that position, requiring a walk down the line and, after climbing up them, a good stiff clout with the coal hammer before they will drop to the 'on' position; water taps frozen, entailing a couple of hundred yards' walk to the next nearest tap, and a fire that refuses to burn in spite of the generous amount of paraffin you feed it. But when at last it does burn and the kettle is boiling and platelayers have arrived to salt the points, you settle down with a mug of tea and the morning paper, not really wishing to be anywhere else.

But most of these people, talking honestly about their jobs, don't even seem to get that kind of consolation. A factory worker says, 'For eight hours a day, five days a week, I'm the exception to the rule that life can't exist in a vacuum. Work to me is a void, and I begrudge every precious minute of my time that it takes.' A man from the printing trade says, 'Now there is little interest in the job other than getting your money on Friday and getting out of the building as fast as you can.'

A nightwatchman says, 'Often before I had felt fed up with jobs, and with work as such, like most other people. But it had been nothing like this. In a strange paradox, by choosing a job which had appeared the most empty, the simplest – the least work-like – I had arrived at the most absolute revulsion against even the notion of any kind of labour.' A clerk says,

One occupational hazard facing a clerk is always the sense of futility he struggles against, or is more often just overwhelmed by. Unlike even the humblest worker on a production line, he doesn't produce *anything*. He battles with phantoms, abstracts: runs a paper chase that goes on year after year, and seems utterly pointless. How can there be anything else other than boredom in it for him?

And a worker on a production line says, 'If you didn't dream at work it would send you mad. It isn't the actual work that kills you in a factory. It's the *repetition*.'

An advertising copy-writer, guilty at earning so much just for writing the ads says, 'Every time I'm asked to write the label for a can of beans I feel absurd. And every time my cheque arrives I'm glad I'm not earning as little as the girl who worked the machine that put the beans in the tin.'

Even people with the kind of job that most of us would think rather glamorous, or at least varied, write with a kind of hatred of their jobs. Thus a house-surgeon says, 'Done properly, the work is the nearest thing to voluntary slavery I can think of.' And a journalist asks,

What were we working for anyway? The short answer was money and everyone knew it. For want of another solution I came to see money as the only possible compensation for eight hours at work. Making them pay for keeping me there, the same money was the means to buying oblivion the rest of the time.

What they are all saying is WORK IS A . . .

. . . BORE

Down the centre of the factory floor there were about twenty talcum-powder-top perforating machines, behind each sat a man on a stool, his hand on the weighted swivel handle. To one side of each man there was a huge tea-chest full of unperforated talcum-powder-tops and to the other a second tea-chest in which to deposit the talcum-powder-tops once they had been perforated. It was work that could have been done by a child of five with Herculean muscles in his right arm – strength was needed but no brain power. The perforating operation was executed as follows: take unperforated top from box, place on press, pull weighted swivel handle towards operator, let go handle which automatically returns to neutral position, take now perforated talcum top from press, place in second tea-chest. Repeat operation *ad infinitum*. A proficient operator was able to perforate about twenty-five tops per minute, though at this speed care had to be taken not to inadvertently perforate the back of the hand. Though I became quite fast I never reached Olympic standard. My mind was far too preoccupied with thoughts of the exotic bathrooms that my finished products would grace, and of the beautiful women who would sprinkle their nude bodies with its sweet-smelling contents. Sometimes I would mentally name the girl whom I would most like to have each of my completed tops. It passed the time and seemed to fit into the rhythm of the work. Christian name (put the top on the press) Surname (pull the handle, let it go and dispose of finished product). Jane Russell, Rita Hayworth, Dorothy Lamour, Jan Sterling, Veronica Lake, Betty Grable, Anna Stern, Ginger Rogers, Katharine Hepburn, Margaret Lockwood, Madeleine Carroll and always Loretta Young – for her I would have liked to have been working in a soap factory. Or better still been a sponge diver in the South Seas.

from *Banana Boy* by Frank Norman

Do you think these women are really 'bored to tears'? They certainly look happy enough. No one could envy them their jobs, but it wouldn't be difficult to think of other ways of spending your working life that would be far more depressing and humiliating than these.
And making up a light-hearted competition about boring jobs brings out the wider problem of what to do about dull, dispiriting work. Do we joke about it – and so try and forget it, or at least glamorize it? Or do we try to find ways of making the job itself more interesting?

BORED

But, Mrs Woodrow, you're the winner

HERE SHE IS–the woman with the most boring job in Britain. Her name: Mrs. Brenda Woodrow.

Her job: peeling onions, six hours a day, five days a week.

It's enough to make a saint weep. And Mrs. Woodrow, who is twenty-one and lives in Foxley-road, Foulsham, Norfolk, DOES weep every day when she starts sorting out the pickling onions.

Mrs. Woodrow was chosen from thousands of entries to the Mirror's "Boring Jobs" competition, which sprang from a recent statement by Prince Philip that women could cope with humdrum jobs better than men.

Mrs. Woodrow's winning entry read:

"Yes, tears often come to my eyes. I sit in the same place next to the same person. Six hours a day, five days a week. For the past two and a half years. My job? Peeling onions!"

Now she gets her reward. Mrs. Woodrow and her husband George, 25, will be guests of the Daily Mirror on a super day out in London. It will be a real outing to remember, for Brenda has never been to London.

Says George: "When she first started the job the smell she brought home was something wicked. But now I've got used to it. Sometimes I catch a whiff from her hair when we get into bed, but it is not too bad."

So that's the winner. But there were plenty of other ladies who were bored to tears. Here's a selection:

- **I WORK** in a chocolate factory and from 8 a.m. to 5 p.m. each day all I do is stand by a conveyor belt with a brush in my hand and **DUST** the chocolates as they roll past me.—**(Miss) Theresa Hicks, Hornsey, London, N.8.**

- **HOW** about this for a boring, dead-end job? I am a cleaner at the local crematorium. At least no one complains.—**(Mrs.) V. Park, Cwmbran, Monmouthshire.**

- **I AM** a traffic crossing keeper for British Rail and have to open and shut two heavy gates every time a vehicle wants to cross over the lines. I do nothing but go back and forward pushing these gates from 6.15 a.m. to 11 p.m. seven days a week. On top of it all, a warning bell rings in my house every time a train is coming into the station.—**(Mrs.) E. Mohammed, The Grove, Rye, Sussex.**

- **I DRIVE** round in a van from 7.30 a.m. to 5 p.m. daily calling at each of this town's public loos. I've been cleaning them for eighteen years and am bored stiff with the sight of those forty-six lavatory pans and ten washbasins. What's more I'll be doing exactly the same on Christmas Day.—**(Miss) L. Turner, Ramsgate, Kent.**

All the ladies mentioned on these pages will get a cheque for three guineas—with the compliments of the Daily Mirror.

MISS WEBSTER—she's been two years in a factory that makes women's vests.

GOING DOTTY

"I THINK my job is very boring as all I do is to put dots on the backs of vests with a pencil."

(Miss) Phyllis Webster, Whitfield-avenue, Glossop, Derbyshire.

And five wh

THE SCREAMERS (left to right): Hilda Jennings, R

TO TEARS!

NDA WOODROW—knowing her onions

re screaming with frustration

s, Gwen Baker, Margaret Vyse and Judy Palin.

WE work in very hot conditions. We stare through a tinted square of glass and weld, helping to make the best cars in the world, Rolls-Royces. Our job is so boring and frustrating.

If we didn't stop occasionally and scream at the top of our voices, bang things, throw things and kick things, we would all be in a hypnotic trance.

No, we don't get into trouble. The foreman and workmates carry on as if nothing was wrong. They know what we are going through.

Margaret Vyse, Gwen Baker, Rose Yates, Judy Palin, Hilda Jennings, 135 Department, Rolls-Royce Ltd., Crewe, Cheshire.

MISS JARVIS—not moving a muscle.

UN-BARE-ABLE

WHAT do I do? Absolutely nothing. All I do to earn my daily bread is to keep quite still, not move a muscle—for hours on end. Nothing on either. Pardon? Oh, I'm an art college model.

(Miss) Rose-Marie Jarvis, Baker-street, Nottingham.

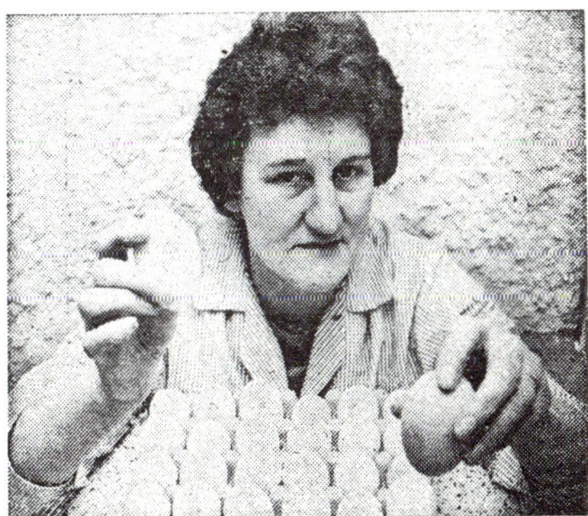

MRS. YOUNG—eggs from 60,000 battery hens.

EGGSASPERATING!

I AM shut in a hen-house on my own, just continually picking up thousands of eggs. Day in, day out, even Bank Holidays. The eggs can't be left.

(Mrs.) Bertha Young, Catbrook, near Chepstow, Mon.

A woman's work is not much fun

Most women who work hold down two jobs. One they get paid for, and the other starts when they get home from their paid job and stops when they go back to it.

But what about the wife who stays at home? How much would she earn if she had to be paid the rate for the job?

In 1971 a divorce court judge estimated the value of a wife to her family at fifty pence an hour. This led Yvonne Thomas to do some calculating:

The judge's estimate could be considered a little on the mean side, even if 50p an hour is the best going rate for a charwoman or baby-sitter in London.

If you are going to say how much a wife is worth in cash terms, the only fair way is to break down what she does, and pay her the rates. To be fair, take an average wife with an average family of two children (the wife Justice Talbot valued at 50p an hour had five).

She gets up fairly early in the morning, say 7.30, and spends half an hour getting breakfast for the family. Then she spends twenty minutes taking the children to school. Arriving home by 9.30, she could perhaps put her feet up for half an hour, then spend from ten o'clock to 1 p.m. cleaning out the house. From one to two lunch break, then a couple of hours' shopping before collecting the children from school at 4 p.m.

Another twenty minutes getting home, then she makes tea and gives it to them, clears up and starts to think of cooking her husband's evening meal. Between times she may do gardening or laundry or some minor nursing or other odd jobs.

Since, when you evaluate a wife in this way you have to be very mercenary about it, you need to know the proper rate for each job.

In London a charwoman can get as much as 50p an hour, and this is what some domestic agencies charge. Council welfare departments will supply home helps to assist old people and others in need at less. A home help in Westminster receives 38p an hour – a little less than a home help in Hounslow who gets 39p an hour.

There are other agencies where you can hire women to do specific jobs, like washing up after lunch or dinner: £2·63. A parlourmaid who will lay the table, serve the meal (not cook it), clear and wash up, can be hired for £3·75 from 6 p.m. to 10 p.m. You can hire a 'proxy parent' – a stand-in Ma – at £14 a week plus keep and expenses, but you can't expect her to be quite as tolerant as a real mother.

For taking the kids to and from school, a child escort could be hired at £1 an hour; or if you want to have the child taken to granny's the other side of town, your hired escort will do it, plus expenses, at £1 for each of the first eight hours, 75p thereafter.

You could be lucky with the part-time gardener and undercut the rates by getting a sprightly pensioner to cut the lawn at 50p an hour. Could be three times as much by a professional firm.

If anyone falls sick, you need a nurse. If it is serious, £5 a day and keep for a State Registered Nurse. But if merely sensible home nursing is needed, a nursing auxiliary can be hired at 45p an hour, or £3·80 a day. A nursery nurse to take care of the baby or the small children will cost £17 to £21 plus accommodation and food a week if it is a temporary job or about a fiver less if you are offering permanent work. For that you will get someone who can handle babies properly – just about as well as a real mother.

If you want to be really penny-pinching you could claim a chauffeuse (say £1 an hour at a conservative rate) and someone to darn socks. And if you are desperate, dial Help for the Day – and get a prayer by telephone.

THE COST OF A WIFE'S JOB
7.30 AM GET UP
8 TO 8.30 MAKE BREAKFAST – ½ HOUR AT 50P PER HOUR
8.40 TO 9 AM TAKE CHILDREN TO SCHOOL – £1 PER HOUR
9–9.20 RETURN HOME – £1 PER HOUR
9.20 TO 10 REST
10 AM TO 1 PM : CLEANING 50P PER HOUR
2 TO 4 PM SHOPPING – 50P PER HOUR
KLEEN
YUMMY CHO
4.30 TO 5.15 : MAKE AND CLEAR TEA 50P PER HOUR
4 TO 4.30 PM COLLECT CHILDREN FROM SCHOOL AND BACK 66P.
6 TO 7 PM WASH AND PUT CHILDREN TO BED – 45P PER HOUR
7.30 TO 8.30 MAKE EVENING MEAL 45P PER HOUR
7 TO 10 PM : LAY TABLE, CLEAR, WASH UP, TIDY UP £3.75P
TOTAL COST £9.09 AND THIS EXCLUDES THE COST OF GARDENING, DECORATING THE HOUSE, NURSING.....AND THE WEAR AND TEAR OF PUTTING UP WITH THE FAMILY SEVEN DAYS A WEEK.

WORKERS should be given "think breaks" as well as tea breaks, says psychologist George Hall.

The minutes of meditation would not be allowed to develop into an excuse for a chat and a cigarette.

All work would stop, and everyone from the management down would sit still and have a good ponder on the job—how to improve it and how to be happier at it.

Not exactly a think break, but at least a short stretch. Once an hour in this Japanese transistor factory a loudspeaker calls out: 'Stop working . . . take a deep breath . . . one, two, three, four. . . .' The assembly-line workers comply with a mass yawn and stretch.

Down tools!

One hundred and forty years ago, William Benbow, shoemaker and café owner, issued a pamphlet from his Commercial Coffee House in London, with the title

GRAND NATIONAL HOLIDAY
AND CONGRESS OF
THE PRODUCTIVE CLASSES

In it he argued that although the work of the mass of the people was the only source of wealth, a much smaller number of people, a privileged few, were the only people to benefit from it. How had this become possible? he asked. And he answered that it was because of the ignorance and lack of unity among the people. And how could they get the just rewards of their labour? By uniting, stopping work and proclaiming a national holiday for a month. The very act of stopping work would make people conscious of their strength, and of the power of their united action. 'The month's holiday must be a month's Congress of the working men; a people's month for taking stock of the social conditions.'

It never happened, of course, and even though a General Strike did come nearly a hundred years later, it wasn't quite the National Holiday that Benbow had in mind. Strikes with much more modest aims are always happening, and quite often they achieve their aims.

They usually, but by no means always, happen because the workers concerned want more money, and have found by experience that the best way to get it is to down tools and wait for results. To wish that strikes did not happen is to wish that human beings were a different kind of animal. The only industrial countries where strikes do not happen are the most ruthless dictatorships.

But there are some jobs in this country, in which strikes are illegal. Can you name them? And what do the workers in these jobs do, as a last resort, if they do not think they are getting a square deal?

The more vital the job to the rest of society, the more inconvenience and hardship is caused to other people if the workers in these jobs decide to down tools or to go slow. What happened when the dustmen, the sewer-workers and the gravediggers went on strike, and when the power-station workers worked to rule? The newspapers were full of stories of the hardship and suffering caused, but nobody takes much notice when journalists go on strike. The 'revolt of the dogsbodies' happened because workers in lowly paid, but absolutely vital jobs, saw everybody else keeping up with the cost of living, while they got left behind.

But not all strikes are about money. Some psychologists think that, even when the arguments are about pay, the real reasons are quite different. They see strikes as a necessary safety valve for the pent-up feelings of frustration which most people have about their jobs. And they point out that days lost through strikes vary from industry to industry and from firm to firm, alongside days lost through other reasons: sickness for example.

Dr Peter Taylor of the TUC Institute of Occupational Health studied absence from work through sickness in several countries and found a steady increase in all the Western industrial countries. He concluded that in all 'advanced' societies 'there has been a definite change of national or individual thresholds in terms of the amount of ill health which people are prepared to tolerate'. Could it be that there is also a threshold in the amount of frustration at work that people can tolerate, and that there comes a point at which we lose our tempers and down tools?

Days lost through strikes: 11 million
Days lost through sickness and accidents: 311 million

Talking point

Strikes – part of the high power cycle?

The alternation of record output figures with strikes and working-to-rule has increasingly taken on the look of a two-stroke power cycle. An industrial dispute is a drawing in of the energy available to the workers in preparation for a subsequent power stroke. . . . A strike can provide the emotional excitement, the challenge, the idealism, the competitiveness and the direct monetary commitment which repetition work in an automated factory completely fails to do.

from a letter to *The Times*

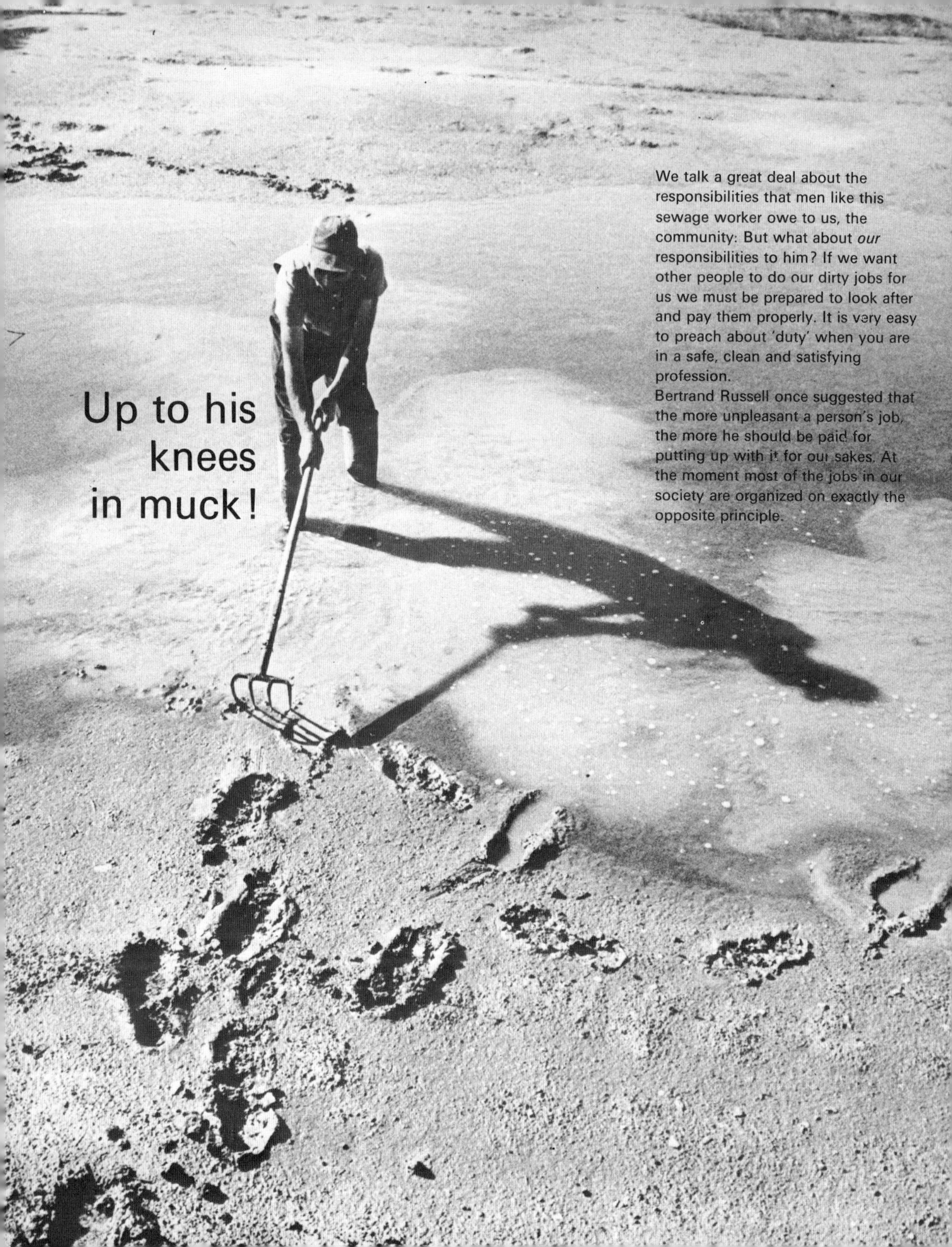

Up to his knees in muck!

We talk a great deal about the responsibilities that men like this sewage worker owe to us, the community: But what about *our* responsibilities to him? If we want other people to do our dirty jobs for us we must be prepared to look after and pay them properly. It is very easy to preach about 'duty' when you are in a safe, clean and satisfying profession.

Bertrand Russell once suggested that the more unpleasant a person's job, the more he should be paid for putting up with it for our sakes. At the moment most of the jobs in our society are organized on exactly the opposite principle.

Not enough man's work?

It's hard to grow up when there isn't enough man's work. . . . There get to be fewer jobs that are necessary or unquestionably useful; that require energy and draw on some of one's best capacities; and that can be done keeping one's honour and dignity.

By 'man's work' I mean a very simple idea, so simple that it is clearer to ingenuous boys than to most adults. To produce necessary food and shelter is man's work. During most of economic history most men have done this drudging work, secure that it was justified and worthy of a man to do it, though often feeling that the social conditions under which they did it were *not* worthy of a man, thinking, 'It's better to die than to live so hard' – but they worked on. When the environment is forbidding, as in the Swiss Alps or the Aran Islands, we regard such work with poetic awe. In emergencies it is heroic, as when the bakers of Paris maintained the supply of bread during the French Revolution, or the milkmen did not miss a day's delivery when the bombs recently tore up London.

At present there is little such substance work. I guess that one-tenth of our economy is devoted to it; it is more likely one-twentieth. Production of food is actually discouraged. Farmers are not wanted and the young men go elsewhere. Building, on the contrary is immensely needed. New York City needs 65,000 new units a year, and is getting 16,000. One would think that ambitious boys would flock to this work. But here we find that building, too, is discouraged. In a great city, for the last twenty years hundreds of thousands have been ill housed, yet we do not see science, industry and labour enthusiastically enlisted to find the quick solution to a definite problem. . . . None of these people is much interested in providing shelter, and nobody is at all interested in providing new manly jobs.

from *Growing Up Absurd* by Paul Goodman

On artisans

While those with vested interests in bloating our educational system make much moan about the vacant places in our universities, common men may take comfort from contemplating the wisdom of the chairman of the Bagshot Rural Council. In attending a local school prize-giving he sagely told the children that though many would want to be scientists and go to the Moon, there was still an opportunity in the ordinary, earthbound jobs of motor mechanics, carpenters and bricklayers. "Your wages may not compare very favourably with others while you are training", he said, "but I predict in the future your skill will be so much in demand that you will be gold dust."

As more and more people become redundantly over-educated and prevented by intellectual pride from using anything but their brains, so will rise the economic value of that manual elite who can effectively use their hands. It may be profitable for the percipient of our younger generation to ponder well the advice from Bagshot. After all, what will it profit a nation if it has a multitude of academics who can distinguish a quasar from a maser and estimate the mass of a neutrino, if there is nobody around to empty the dustbins, mend the pipes, fix the roof or instal the lavatories? Knowledge may possibly be power but there's certainly going to be gold, my boy, in them thar horny hands.

from *New Scientist*

3 LIVING WITHOUT WORK

Ginger Mills

In Vancouver they have a Town Fool, who lives on a grant from the Canada Council and sits on the steps of the Law Courts, talking to whoever will listen. And in Hertfordshire there is Ginger Mills, wildman of St Albans. Jeff Cloves, who used to produce a magazine there, wrote this poem about him (and says that 'Ginge, like the true artist he is, was buying copies from me at a tanner and selling them for two bob').

In the Summer
you are a tourist attraction.
Their illustrated guides
have not prepared them for
The Wildman of St Albans
with tanned bare chest
and pelt of red hair
and a spangled aboriginal
stomping among the
brittle relics
of Centurions and Abbots
is not to be missed.
But how do you survive
the Winter
Ginger?
Do you lay up
in that tent they say is your
home,
carving wooden totems
and stalking out
into the still morning
countryside
to lift a frosty hare
from your expert snare?
Do you hibernate in your
sleeping bag
and dream
you gallop with furry Cossacks
across the Russian plains
and migrate with the hunting
tribes
to Summer prairies
and run before the trades
in endless tropic seas?
Or do you ride out the Winter
on the dole
crouching each day
over the juke box
down at Jacks,
drearily
awaiting the Spring.

Who can say?

The Town abounds
in fantastic legends
of your deeds
and everybody knows you
and has a tale
to add. . . .
For you are
OUR Wildman
OUR Magician
OUR Talisman.
But your ways remain
a mystery.

At Dusk
The Wildman slopes by
deep in sleepy shadows,
drifts into the dark
behind close hedges,
flits over fields
under the growing moon,
enters
his own world.
Your own world
Ginger?

No one leaves space
for the likes of you

anymore
and the daily spread
of concrete
pushes you farther back.
When the Builder
bribes
another field or two
from the Farmer
and the country town
expands
no thought is spared
for the tracks
of the Wildman.

But you survive
and so do we.
On the edge of the town
where fields were just
five years ago
we pattern our lives to fit
our raw estate
while you
hack out your weird and
secret life
beyond the rim of our
ordered existence.
Living out your dreams

you dare
where we dread,
but no sense of menace
of threat
or fear
surrounds you
and a meeting on the pavement
is an encounter
with the strange
but not the terrible.

from *A true legend of Ginger Mills* by Jeff Cloves

All in a day's work 2 ***The Royal family***
Living out other people's dreams – for a million a year?

On the dole

When I first saw unemployed men at close quarters, the thing that horrified and amazed me was to find that many of them were *ashamed* of being unemployed. I was very ignorant, but not so ignorant as to imagine that when the loss of foreign markets pushes two million men out of work, those two million are any more to blame than the people who draw blanks in the Calcutta Sweep. But at that time nobody cared to admit that unemployment was inevitable, because this meant admitting that it would probably continue. The middle classes were still talking about 'lazy idle loafers on the dole' and saying that 'these men could all find work if they wanted to', and naturally these opinions percolated to the working class themselves. I remember the shock of astonishment it gave me, when I first mingled with tramps and beggars, to find that a fair proportion, perhaps a quarter, of these beings whom I had been taught to regard as cynical parasites, were decent young miners and cotton-workers gazing at their destiny with the same sort of dumb amazement as an animal in a trap. They simply could not understand what was happening to them. They had been brought up to work, and behold! it seemed as if they were never going to have the chance of working again. In their circumstances it was inevitable, at first, that they should be haunted by a feeling of personal degradation. That was the attitude towards unemployment in those days: it was a disaster which happened to *you* as an individual and for which you were to blame.

from *The Road to Wigan Pier* by George Orwell (1937)

Not so different? Walter Hood, unemployed in 1930, drew this in 1970.

	1930s	1970s
STAGE ONE	When a man fell out of work he would, on the first day, dress in his Sunday suit with collar and tie. He shaved, pinned on his ex-serviceman's badge and, head held high, lined up at the labour exchange. He kept up his spirits by joking with his mates, the whole works or coal mine having shut down at once.	They'd made him redundant the previous week but he was going to get another job, definitely, just to show them. Most of them start off angry. Their pride is so hurt that they're furious. They rush in and out of dole queues, arguing with the staff.
STAGE TWO	As the weeks passed, the unemployed man changed. He stopped dressing up. He acquired a characteristic slouch, the result of hanging around street corners with his hands in his pockets. He left the stubble on his cheeks.	After six months they calm down as the dole becomes routine and they work out their own philosophies. 'Life is not work and work is not life,' said a thirty-five-year-old man in the queue at South Shields. 'It's both. But if I went to Nottingham, I'd lose half my life because I belong here.'
STAGE THREE	As the months passed his hands grew white – softer and whiter than those of his wife. He saw grass grow in the derelict place where he used to work. As the alternative to standing in the street, he might shuffle into the library reading room to look at magazine pictures of society beauties. As the years passed, the unemployed man turned grey. Everyone commented on the greyness of the hard core unemployed – grey hair, grey stubble, even grey skin. He seemed to be looking at the ground all the time. He wore incongruous clothes, perhaps pin-striped trousers cast off and given to charity by a bank manager. He felt he had no dignity. He knew he had no hope. from *The Slump* by Colin Cross	The third stage is apathy which gets worse as the years roll by. They begin to believe they're failures and there's no point in anything. But unlike the Thirties, there are no physical hardships. The dole keeps everyone alive, just. 'I don't think the money they give you does let you live,' said a woman in Durham. 'All it lets you do is linger.' These emotional and mental hardships can be far worse than the physical. In every dole queue there are young hippie types, all on the dole themselves, giving out leaflets, trying to stir up enthusiasm for a repetition of the Jarrow marches. But nobody is interested in marching. Nobody is hungry. The dole has saved them and beaten them at the same time. from 'On the Dole '71' by Hunter Davies, *Sunday Times*, 21 March 1971

Tom Pickard, became, by the age of twenty-two 'the poet laureate of the city of Newcastle'. He rented the Medieval Morden Tower for ten shillings a week to hold poetry readings for young people in the city. Soon it was visited by famous poets from both sides of the Atlantic and, after much wrangling with committees, Tom became the only English poet subsidized by the ratepayers, while the Tower was publicized as a tourist attraction for foreign visitors. A few years earlier, when he was eighteen, he wrote this account of what it felt like to be an unemployed teenager.

"Say, Bill, work's that scarce now they're selling it!"

I have been unemployed for nearly two years. Since I left school I have had two jobs, one in a warehouse, this lasted for nine months before I was fired, the other was at Woolworths. I was there for two months, and along with five others was sacked for slacking.

It is a pleasant experience to be on the dole for this period of time, though it has its disadvantages; I mean when I want a job, and this often happens – you miss the pick-in-the-hand feeling and the smell of the factory etc. (I think it's your mates you miss most.) Of course you forget the clocking-in and the captivity bits – but then you want the job because the lass is up the stick or something, and you can't get it. Usually though, when they are there to get, the wages are so poor for lads that I prefer my dole money.

And if I seriously wanted a job I couldn't get one because of my record (which is not half as bad as some of the other lads' are).

Q How many jobs have you had?
A Two. One at Finneys Seeds and one at Woolworths.
Q Why did you leave?
A I didn't. I got fired.
Q From both?
A Yes.
Q How long have you been unemployed?
A Two years this Christmas.
Q Which school and what standard achieved?
A Firefield Sec. Mod. and I didn't take any exams because I was in the 'D Form' all the way through.

Most of the interviews I've had have taken this form, and I never got the job. Another disadvantage is the National Assistance Board. As soon as I applied for National Assistance they sent an inspector who comes snooping, makes snide comments about us not being married, and suggests I move on to another district in search of work. . . . Move on to another parish. . . . That suggestion is mad. Tyneside is not the only black spot.

Snide things happen all the time on the dole, things which no one does anything about. Employers have a choice of a dozen lads, and therefore offer a very low price – knowing that someone will take it. They know that pressure from parents – who want their kids working no matter what – gives them the opportunity to fix wages to their own liking.

Lots of lads hate being on the dole, because to many of them it means being out of pocket. The boys who have just left school and are entitled to no money because they've paid no stamps, and are too young to claim assistance, will jump at the chance of any job. These are the lads who the car-wash firms are aiming at.

Every time I have been offered work at the dole, one of the jobs will be car-washing. If at any time I go in and ask what they have, car-washing will always be mentioned. All the lads who have been on the dole for long will avoid the car-wash firms. In any case it is the lads of fifteen who are preferred. They can be paid the lowest wages – £2 17s. (1963). The hours are long

The Depression. It loomed so large in ordinary people's lives that they even sent postcards about it.

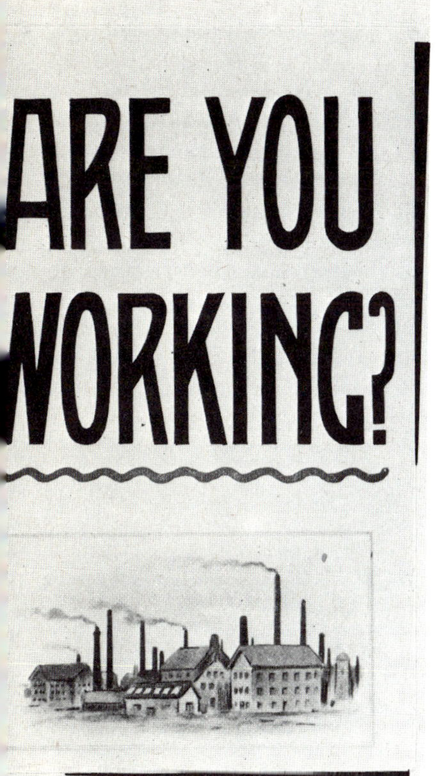

The New Leader

A. J. COOK'S NARRATIVE

Price Twopence

The New Leader

VOL. XIII. No. 35.

FRIDAY, JUNE 11, 1926

Registered at the G.P.O. as a Newspaper

FLAMBO

The Shadow of Hunger

Have you done your duty by contributing to the Miners' Fund?

and the breaks short. Half an hour for lunch. They are expected to work alternate weekends. The job is very heavy and most of the boys can't stick it very long – but the money is better than they would get on the dole.

Usually after a week they are fired for skiving, i.e. resting, or have had all they can stick, and hand their notice in, which means they are on the dole again with no or little benefit. Usually most lads hand in their cards and so are not entitled to benefit for six weeks.

Once again they are at home during the day, being nagged at by their mothers for giving the job up, and for living off her. So the chances that they will take another dead-end racket job, when it comes along, are increased.

Obviously as more kids leave school and fall into similar situations, the exploitation of the unemployed will continue. The Youth Employment Officers take little interest in this sort of thing and *no* action against it. I have heard an employer complaining over the phone that the boys sent to him were not suitable for the situation, and as a ratepayer he was being badly done to. The poor – wants his labourers with degrees. 'I herewith return goods stamped not suitable. In future please send me best stock.'

from 'Teenage unemployment – what it really feels like' by Tom Pickard (*Anarchy* 34, 1963)

There are some jobs which are more like play than work. They are like a game that some people are lucky enough to get paid for playing. The stage and film director Peter Hall, for example, says, 'unless I can play at my work, I'm useless'. How different from the jobs that most people do for a living. But no one would suffer if it wasn't done. And the kind of fun-work that hippies approve of is the kind that most people wouldn't miss. Some worker who hasn't got the message slaves away in a sweaty papermill to produce the paper used by the underground porn industry, someone far away is growing the brown rice that is served in the underground restaurant, someone made the cloth they wear, built the houses they inhabit.

It's because you're part of the system even if you only live off it, that some drop-outs from the world of work move right out to make their own system. At Drop City, Colorado, they build their homes in domes, built from the junk and scrap that rich America throws away. Bill Voyd, who lives there, describes the shock of giving up work:

Most people, when they first come to Drop City, do not know what to do with themselves. We lead a day-to-day existence, functioning within a loose structure, almost invisible most of the time, a structure that is always growing and shifting and changing as we change. We have no compulsory work. So a new person to arrive is often faced with a problem: his survival is provided for; all his time is free time – what is he going to do with it?

He often vacillates between great flurries of activity and depressions of nothingness. Having been pigeon-holed all his life, man does not know what to do with his freedom. We call this 'cultural shock'. But sooner or later most begin to settle into a rhythm – each into his own natural rhythm. Since there are no compulsions, each eventually discovers how he wants to lead his life. Or life begins – in spite of his protestations – to lead him. He becomes the person he really is by doing the things he wants to do. All activity is creative activity. All creative activity is done for its own sake, without ends. All non-compulsory activity is art.

'Why don't you get a job driving one of the big trucks along here?'

'I don't like what's in the boxes,' said Horatio sadly. 'It could just as well drop in the river – and I'd make mistakes and drop it there.'

'Is it bad stuff?'

'No, just useless. It takes the heart out of me to work at something useless and I begin to make mistakes. I don't mind putting profits in somebody's pocket – but the job also has to be useful for something.'

'Why don't you go to the woods and be a lumberjack?'

'No! They chop down the trees just to print off the *New York Times!*'

from *The Empire City* by Paul Goodman

4 THE FUTURE OF WORK

The future of work – seen from the past

Now as to the work, first of all it will be useful, and, therefore, honourable and honoured; because there will be no temptation to make mere useless toys, since there will be no rich men cudgelling their brains for means for spending superfluous money, and consequently no 'organizers of labour' pandering to degrading follies for the sake of profit, wasting their intelligence and energy in contriving snares for cash in the shape of trumpery which they themselves heartily despise. Nor will the work turn out trash; there will be no millions of poor to make a market for wares which no one would choose to use if he were not driven to do so; everyone will be able to afford things good of their kind, and will have knowledge enough to reject what is not excellent; coarse and rough wares may be made for temporary purposes, but they will openly proclaim themselves for what they are; adulteration will be unknown.

Furthermore, machines of the most ingenious and

The rhythm of human activity: barn-raising in nineteenth-century America, and self-raising at the Woodstock Pop Festival.

best-approved kinds will be used when necessary, but will be used simply to save human labour; nor, indeed, could they be used for anything else in such well-ordered work as we are thinking about. . . .

Well, the manufacture of useless goods, whether harmful luxuries for the rich or disgraceful make-shifts for the poor, having come to an end, and we still being in possession of the machines once used for mere profit-grinding, but now used only for saving human labour, it follows that much less labour will be necessary for each workman; all the more as we are going to get rid of all non-workers, and busy-idle people; so that the working time of each member of our factory will be very short, say, to be much within the mark, four hours a day.

Now, next it may be allowable for an artist – that is, one whose ordinary work is pleasant and not slavish – to hope that in no factory will all the work, even that necessary four hours' work, be mere machine-tending; and it follows from what was said above about machines being used to save labour, that there would be no work which would turn men into mere machines; therefore, at least some proportion of the work, the necessary and in fact compulsory work I mean, would be pleasant to do; the machine-tending ought not to require a very long apprenticeship, therefore in no case should any one person be set up to run up and down after a machine through all his working hours every day, even so shortened as we have seen; now the attractive work of our factory, that which was pleasant in itself to do, would be of the nature of art; therefore all slavery of work ceases under such a system, for whatever is burden-some about the factory would be taken turn and turn about, and so distributed, would cease to be a burden – would be, in fact, a kind of rest from the more exciting or artistic work.

from *A Factory As It Might Be*
by William Morris (1884)

Paying men not to work

Major Major's father

He was a long-limbed farmer, a God-fearing, freedom-loving, law-abiding rugged individualist who held that federal aid to anyone but farmers was creeping socialism. He advocated thrift and hard work and disapproved of loose women who turned him down. His speciality was alfalfa, and he made a good thing of not growing any. The government paid him well for every bushel of alfalfa he did not grow. The more alfalfa he did not grow the more money the government gave him, and he spent every penny he didn't earn on new land to increase the amount of alfalfa he did not produce. Major Major's father worked without rest at not growing alfalfa. On long winter evenings he remained indoors and did not mend harness, and he sprang out of bed at the crack of noon every day just to make certain that the chores would not be done. He invested in land wisely and was soon not growing more alfalfa than any other man in the county. Neighbours sought him out for advice on all subjects, for he had made much money and was therefore wise. 'As ye sow, so shall ye reap,' he counselled one and all, and everyone said, 'Amen'.

Major Major's father was an outspoken champion of economy in government, provided it did not interfere with the sacred duty of government to pay farmers as much as they could get for all the alfalfa they produced that no one else wanted, or for not producing any alfalfa at all. He was a proud and independent man who was opposed to unemployment insurance.

from *Catch-22* by Joseph Heller

Major Major's father, in *Catch-22*, is paid by the United States government for *not* farming his land. But this is not the funny thing about him: the funny thing is that he still believes that it is wicked to subsidize idleness, except his own. Since the Second World War the farm labour force in the USA has been reduced from 14 to 7 per cent of the population. Taking into account people who are underemployed, like Major Major's father, or who simply feed themselves, the figure is more like 5 per cent. And the food produced by this 5 per cent is more than can be profitably sold to the other 95 per cent.

What is true of farmers is true of lumberjacks, miners, textile workers, factory workers of every kind, construction workers, storekeepers and clerks. The American government estimates that automation is putting 50,000 more able-bodied men and women out of work each year. Union leaders claim that the figure is closer to 80,000. There are vast numbers of Americans who will never work again. One government economist called them *no-people*. Their labour is neither wanted nor needed: machines will do the work better. They live on relief – on welfare handouts like the dole.

There are two things bad about this *in our society*, and we have seen both of them earlier in this book. The first is that being without work so often destroys your self-confidence and sense of your own dignity. The second is that the dole may stop you from starving, but shuts you out of the good things of life simply because you lack *purchasing power* – you haven't the money to pay for them. It may be that the best things in life are free, but try telling that to a man with no money.

Your lack of purchasing power means that you cannot buy the goods that other workers are producing, and in times of depression that means that they get laid off too. In the slump of the 1930s government efforts to cut down spending only made things worse, and a famous economist J. M. Keynes pointed out that the way to get out of the slump was to spend more, in order to create demand and get the factories going again.

More recently, an American economist J. K. Galbraith has argued for what he calls Cyclically Graduated Compensation – a dole which goes up when times are bad, so that people can go on spending and consequently keep other people employed, and which goes down when full employment is approached. Another American, Robert Theobald, goes further than this, and demands a 'guaranteed annual income' to be paid to every American as a constitutional right. 'One day,' Galbraith says, 'we shall remove the economic penalties and also the social stigma associated with involuntary unemployment. This will make the economy much easier to manage.' But, he adds, 'we haven't done this yet'.

And there isn't any sign of us doing so in Britain either. However, it looks as though something of this kind must happen. And the reason is this. Governments, politicians, employers, managers and efficiency experts all over the world declare that productivity per man hour must be increased, and this depends, as every development in production ever since the industrial revolution has shown, on *the elimination of human labour*. But your income – and consequently your chance of getting the things that money can buy – depends upon your job. We cannot have it both ways. We will have to break the link between jobs and income.

This is why it seems likely that by the time the readers of this book are middle-aged, they will have to be paid a living wage, *whether they work or not*, and that for the first time in human history ordinary people will have the choice which was available only to the rich and powerful in the past: how to spend their time free from the compulsion to work.

Above left: automation has revolutionized the car industry. It has brought down the cost of cars but at what cost to the job interest. *Right*: all industries are liable to become automated. At first sight this looks like a Heath Robinson invention for the most complicated way of laying a brick. But apparently the machine enables bricks to be laid three times as quickly as by hand. Powered by a petrol engine, the machine travels on wheels along tubular rails. Bricks placed in it are lowered into position whilst mortar is fed in from two hoppers. Two labourers keep the machine supplied whilst a third checks the laying of the bricks and attends to the pointing.
Can you think of any hidden ways in which this machine might not be a time-saver, e.g. in the accurate laying of the rails?

If you didn't have to work, how on earth would you spend your time?

There are at least four possibilities, and each of them means a revolution.

1. You might use your new freedom to shop around and swap around among jobs. The revolution this would mean is **the abolition of the division of labour**.
2. You might share out the necessary work so that everyone worked just a few hours, while more and more elaborate forms of leisure would grow up. The leisure industry would expand until you would *have to work* to keep up with your ever-more-expensive leisure. This is the **leisure revolution**.
3. Work and leisure would disappear as separate aspects of life. Work would be another kind of hobby, or another kind of art. This would be the **do-it-yourself revolution**.
4. People would insist on being their own bosses, deciding for themselves what to produce and how to produce it, and for whom to produce it, joining together in the **workers' control revolution**.

Or all these revolutions might come together.

Question marks

? But if nobody *worked* for money would we need to use money any more? Let everything be free? But what about those things which still wouldn't exist in large enough quantities to go round? Perhaps the answer is a double-decker economy. At the bottom the basic things for free: plastic plates, blue jeans, prefabs, push-bike, fish fingers. At the top the rare things for cash: handmade china, suede suits, country cottages, Norton 600s, caviar. But how would you get the cash? Work for it!

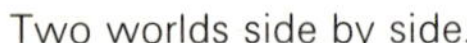

Two worlds side by side.

We can imagine this happening in the rich and technically advanced countries, but what about all the other countries where people would still be desperate for work because a job is a meal ticket? Can you imagine these two worlds existing side by side?

But what about the dirty, dreary jobs? Who will want to do them? In our present-day society there is usually someone who has to take the mucky, ill-paid jobs. Sometimes there already isn't. Birmingham spends £500,000 a year on cleaning up and disposing of litter, but finds it hard to recruit street-sweepers, as an unemployed man with a family gets as much in unemployment pay and family allowances. A society where everyone could get a living without working would either have to mechanize litter-collection, or make street-sweeping a prestige job. Otherwise it would have to put up with its dirt and squalor, or it would have to do its own dirty work with every citizen clearing up his own mess.

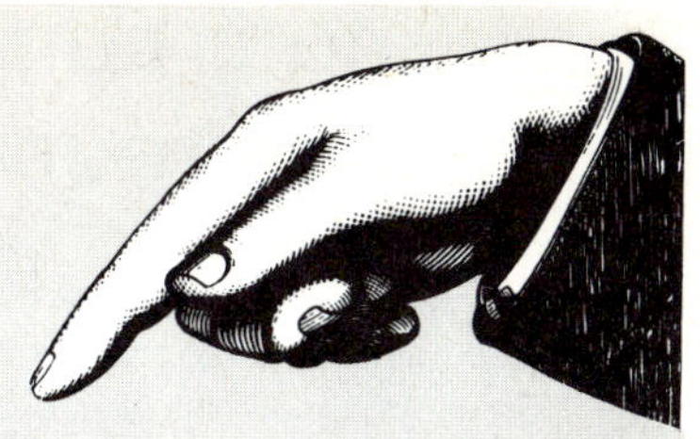

And a warning

. . . it is also imprudent to fall sick or die between 6.00 p.m. on a Friday evening and 9.00 a.m. on a Monday morning. If you felt sick between those hours, you may get no medical attention; and if, in consequence, you die, you will certainly not be able to get yourself buried till Monday comes. Translate this meticulous two days' blackout into a five days' one, and you have the world of the future. . . . Even if the workers' two-day stints are staggered to cover all seven days of the week, they will cover them so thinly that the affluent world will still be a most inconvenient and uncomfortable world to live in.

from *Change and Habit* by Arnold J. Toynbee

Clean it up yourself Mr!

Shopping around swapping around

The division of labour

To take an example from a very trifling manufacture; but one in which the division of labour has been very often taken notice of, the trade of the pin-maker; a workman not educated to this business (which the division of labour has rendered a distinct trade), nor acquainted with the use of the machinery employed in it (to the invention of which the same division of labour has probably given occasion), could scarce, perhaps, with his utmost industry, make one pin in a day, and certainly could not make twenty. But in the way in which this business is now carried on, not only the whole work is a peculiar trade, but it is divided between a number of branches, of which the greater part are likewise peculiar trades. One man draws out the wire, another straightens it, a third cuts it, a fourth points it, a fifth grinds it and the top for receiving the head; to make the head requires two or three distinct operations; to put it on is a peculiar business, to whiten the pins is another; it is even a trade by itself to put them into the paper; and the important business of making a pin is, in this manner, divided into about eighteen distinct operations, which, in some manufactories, are all performed by distinct hands though in others the same man will sometimes perform two or three of them. I have seen a small manufactory of this kind where ten men only were employed, and where some of them consequently performed two or three distinct operations. But although they were very poor, and therefore but indifferently accommodated with the necessary machinery, they could, when they exerted themselves, make among them about twelve pounds of pins in a day. There are in a pound upwards of four thousand pins of a middling size. Those ten persons, therefore, could make among them upwards of forty-eight thousand pins in a day. Each person therefore, making a tenth part of forty-eight thousand pins, might be considered as making four thousand eight hundred pins in a day. But if they had all wrought separately and independently, and without any of them having been educated to this peculiar business, they certainly could not each of them have made twenty, perhaps not one pin in a day; that is, certainly, not the two hundred and fortieth, perhaps not the four thousand eight hundredth part of what they are at present capable of performing, in consequence of a proper division and combination of their different operations.

from *The Wealth of Nations* by Adam Smith, 1776

Above: drawing out wire (2), cutting pin-lengths (3 & 4), pointing pins (7).

Below: heading pins (12 & 13), tin-coating (6 & 7), washing (2), polishing (5).

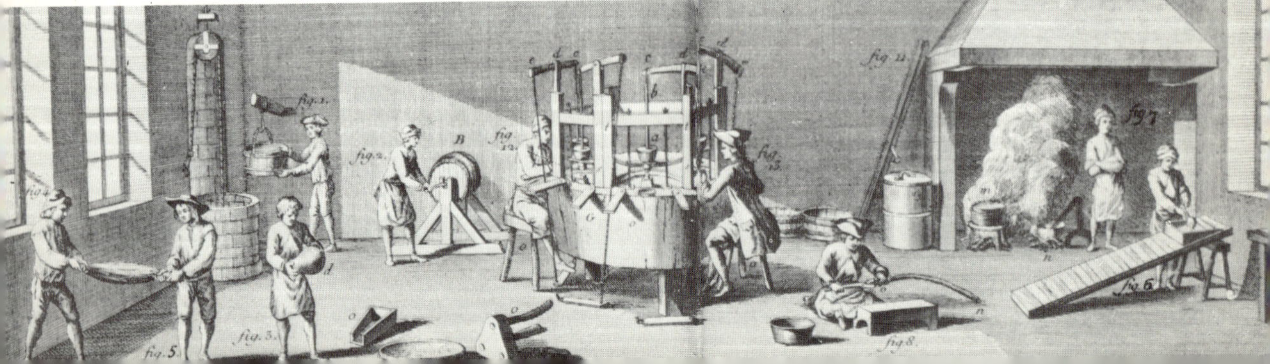

The nine Mexicans in Diego Rivera's drawing can make very many more pots working together and specializing in a particular part of the job, than if each were to knead and shape and decorate the clay and carry it to the kiln and back. The productivity of ancient or modern industry, the possibility of any specialist skill, of every art, and of any spare time for anyone depend on this simple fact. Robinson Crusoe had little leisure. Nearly two hundred years ago Adam Smith worked out the effect of the division of labour in so humble an industry as the making of pins, to demonstrate the point.

But the division of labour, which frees men in some ways enslaves them in others. The boredom of repetition work is one of them, the fact that most people are tied to one kind of job for their working life is another. Karl Marx looked forward to a society which had gone beyond the division of labour:

The division of labour offers us the first example of how, as long as man remains in natural society, that is, as long as a cleavage exists between the particular and the common interest, as long therefore as activity is not voluntarily, but naturally, divided, man's own act becomes an alien power opposed to him, which enslaves him instead of being controlled by him. For as soon as the division of labour begins, each man has a particular, exclusive sphere of activity, which is forced upon him and from which he cannot escape. He is a hunter, a fisherman, a shepherd or a critical critic, and must remain so if he does not want to lose his means of livelihood; whereas in communist society, where nobody has one exclusive sphere of activity but each can become accomplished in any branch he wishes, production as a whole is regulated by society, thus making it possible for me to do one thing today and another tomorrow, to hunt in the morning, fish in the afternoon, rear cattle in the evening, criticize after dinner, in accordance with my inclination, without ever becoming hunter, fisherman, shepherd or critic.

from *The German Ideology* by Karl Marx, 1846

The freedom to shop around and swap around at different jobs that Marx looked forward to hasn't yet arrived for the mass of people in either the East or the West. It is a freedom available today to a clever, versatile or lucky few. The unskilled worker doesn't have it because he can only swap around among unskilled jobs. The ordinary skilled worker doesn't have it because if he doesn't get apprenticed at sixteen or seventeen he doesn't get into the trade, while by the time his apprenticeship is over it is too late for him to change his trade without dropping wages. Very many people start in a job when they leave school and stay in it until they retire.

And then, instead of getting a vote of sympathy for not making the most of their once-and-only life, they get congratulated for their long and faithful service.

Wouldn't it be better and more sensible to have an active job when you are young and vigorous and a comfortable indoor job when you are old and tired? 'When the Gods look down and see the bronzed body of the young labourer they smile. When they see the pale-faced clerk crouched over his desk, they drop tears of sorrow.'

Or wouldn't it be better to have an outdoor job in the summer and an indoor job in the winter, or to do brainwork in the morning and physical work in the afternoon?

But what about the division of labour? What about Adam Smith and his pins? The answer is that the economic laws that belong to a poor society don't necessarily hold good for a rich one. Already industrial psychologists talk about *job enlargement* and *job enrichment*. What they mean is that the breaking down of work into meaningless fragments to increase output can actually reduce production because of the effect on the worker of the mindless repetition work. They have found that giving the worker responsibility for the whole job, not only gives him more satisfaction, but sometimes actually increases production.

Above left: communal living in America demonstrates Marx's idea of people having the opportunity to do a variety of jobs.
Reversing the division of labour has been applied to the Lesney toy factory in England. In the old system (*above*) each worker on the assembly line adds one component to each model car. In the new system shown right one worker assembles a whole car. The rate of production is the same but the new system produces far fewer faulty cars. Why?

Short hours/long leisure

All prophesies about the future predict a tremendous shortening of working hours or days or years. The three-hour day, or the three-day week, or the three-week month, or retirement at fifty – take your pick. It is inevitable, the prophets say, that for most people work is dreary and tedious, but that won't matter in the future because leisure can be long and pleasurable.

To an extent this is what has been happening. The working week in 1850 is estimated to have averaged a little under seventy hours: the equivalent of seven ten-hour days a week or six days of work from six in the morning to six at night.

In Britain, although the unions were demanding an eight-hour day eighty years ago, a report issued in 1971 found factories with a twelve-hour shift system in which employees were working a seventy-two-hour week. It found that more than 250,000 men in this country were working for more than seventy hours a week. It found that, as the standard working week has dropped to forty hours, overtime has increased. In 1947 overtime averaged only one hour a week, but by 1969 it had increased to seven hours. An overwhelming majority of workers interviewed said that they preferred more money to more leisure.

In America the number of people working more than forty-eight hours a week rose from 13 per cent of the work force in 1948 to 20 per cent in 1965, while the number of people who were 'moon-lighting', or holding more than one job, had doubled since 1950.

The reason, of course, is not that people prefer work to leisure, but that in order to enjoy their leisure they feel the need to earn more and therefore to work longer. Or it may be just to get enough to pay the rent.

Certainly leisure is becoming more expensive. People whose grandparents would take the bus to the nearest park on a Sunday, now drive their car to a 'beauty spot' or a 'stately home' – a more costly slice

Leisure activities signposted at a holiday camp.
Will automated industry mean conveyor-belt leisure?

of leisure. Expenditure on cars and motor cycles went up by 600 per cent between 1952 and 1962; expenditure on sailing dinghies went up by 1200 per cent.

The clearest examples of pleasures that are on the increase will be found among activities based on the use of things. The environment of the typical consumer is a dense jungle of things: a house and a summer cottage; cars and a boat; TV, radio and a record player; records, books, newspapers and magazines; clothes and sports clothes; tennis racket, badminton racket, squash racket and table-tennis racket; footballs, beach balls and golf balls. . . . It is the total time spent in using all these things that increases; simultaneously, however, the time allocated to each of them individually is declining.

from *The Harried Leisure Class* by S. B. Linder

In other words, the more of these expensive leisure activities you go in for, the less time you can give to each, and consequently, the more expensive each is in working time to earn the money to pay for the equipment.

There must come a point where the extra pleasure of leisure doesn't quite equal the extra pain of the work needed to buy it.

Thus another American writer James J. Cox says:

Most people feel that the time spent working is lost time – at least lost from conscious enjoyment. But most people have to earn money in order to live. So work is seen as that time the individual must spend in order to achieve the end he seeks – enjoyment. The fact that people see their occupation in this light is largely the *basis* of its registering on the individual as a grind; and the more it grinds, the greater the need for compensatory relief; and the more super-colossal the leisure activities become, the greater the contrast with work and the greater the grind.

What is the relationship of this pattern to the promise of even more leisure? Work hours are crowded into a shorter space of time, becoming distillations of all that work stands for. The two worlds of work and leisure drift farther apart. The recreation world contains all the good, bright, pleasant things, and the work world becomes the dreariest place imaginable. . . .

There are certain basic emotional needs that the individual worker must satisfy. To the degree that the ordinary events of the day are not meeting these needs, recreation serves as a sort of mixture of concentrates to supply these missing satisfactions. When the work experience satisfies virtually none of the requirements, the load on recreation becomes impossible!

All in a day's work 3 A plastic monster maker

Mr Terence Strong was yesterday appointed official dinosaur moulder and assembler to Liverpool Museum.

He was chosen from more than 150 applicants, including twelve teachers, eight engineers, two shipbuilders, two nurses, an occupational therapist, a butcher and a road sweeper.

His job is to recast and assemble the plaster casts of the skeletons of two 150 million year old dinosaurs which the museum has bought from the Museum of Earth Sciences, Utah, for £500 each.

Guardian, 19 May 1971

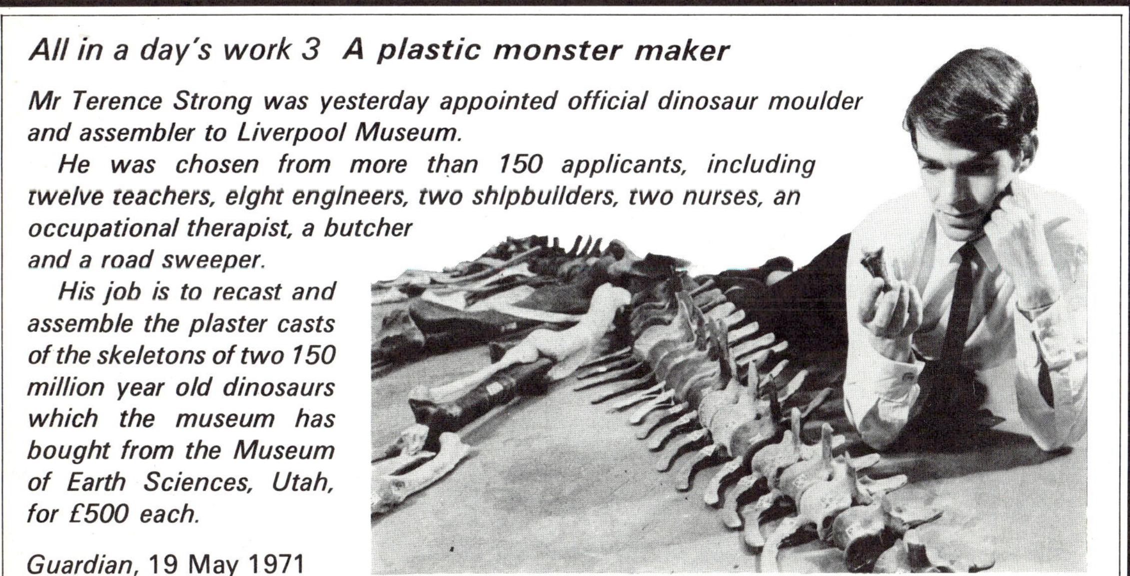

Abolishing the difference between work and leisure

Two men, high up. One repairing his house, the other the Blackpool Tower. We say that one is 'at work' and the other 'making good use of his leisure'. What's the difference?

Much more leisure time than is spent lying in the sun is spent doing things that, if you got paid for them, would be called work, and this simply shows how much we *need* some creative or constructive occupation. The Do-It-Yourself revolution of the last fifteen years hasn't happened just because of the high cost of labour. It has come because people need to *do* something. The government gives a conservative annual figure of £300 million as the annual value of the various do-it-yourself supplies and services sold in this country. You can build your own car, your own fridge or your own house.

Over the past decade there has been a fantastic mushrooming of art-and-crafts hobbies, of photography, home woodwork shops with power tools, ceramics, high fidelity, electronics, radio 'hams'. America has seen the multiplication of the 'amateur' on a scale unknown in previous history. And while this is commendable, it has been achieved at a high cost indeed – the loss of satisfaction in work.

from *Work and its Discontents* by Daniel Bell

Another sociologist, Ferdinand Zweig, questioning car workers in Coventry declares that, 'It is interesting to note that quite often the worker comes to work on Monday worn out from his weekend activities, especially from "do-it-yourself". Quite a number said that the weekend is the most trying and exacting period of the whole week, and Monday work in the factory, in comparison, is relaxing.'

This leads us to ask what *is* work and what *is* leisure, if we work harder at our leisure than at our work. The fact that one of these jobs is paid and the other isn't seems almost beside the point.

Trying to sort out the difference between the two, we can say that, for most people:

WORK IS	**LEISURE IS**
Hated	**Enjoyed**
Long	**Brief**
Paid	**Unpaid**
For someone else	**For yourself**
Essential for livelihood	**Inessential for livelihood**
Concentrated	**At your own pace**
For fixed hours	**In your own time**

SOME PEOPLE DO IT FOR FUN

Which of these pictures is of people working for a living and which is of people doing the same thing for fun? What's the difference?

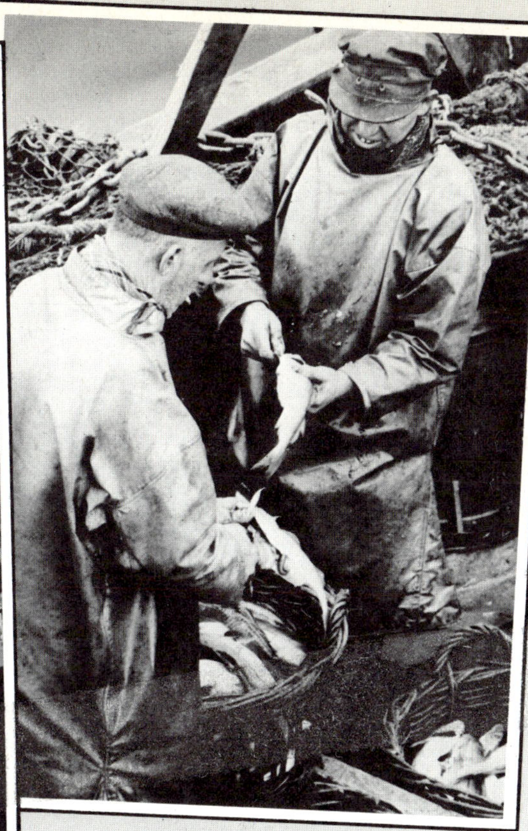

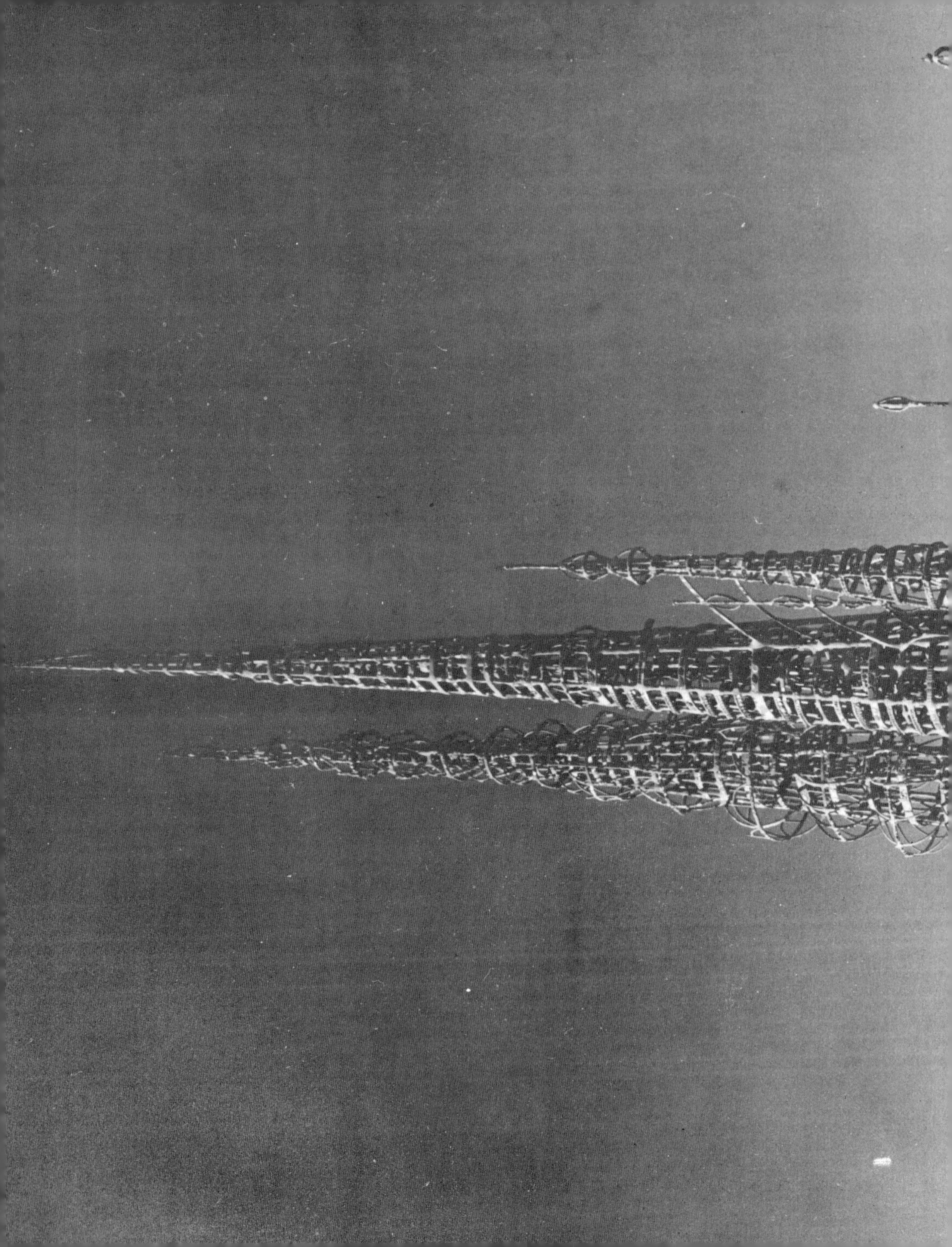

The towers of Watts

Simone Rodilla, called Sam, constructed these towers in thirty-three years (1921–54) in Watts, a small community on the outskirts of Los Angeles. Rodilla, who was born in Italy in the late 1870s, apparently emigrated to the USA around 1900 and soon found work as a skilled tile setter. It is related that when he had settled in Watts and had been able to accumulate some savings, he began in his spare time to erect a monument expressive of his gratitude to America. At the onset of dusk he is supposed to have frequented the huge junk yards of the metropolis with a sack over his shoulder, going there to collect what he needed for his construction: scrap metal, wire, the bottoms of bottles, old and broken dishes, broken glass, shells. Out of iron pieces bent into shapes and then covered with cement, there resulted a structure with extremely varied possibilities of enrichment and decoration. After long and incessant labour, the main tower, which Rodilla built in his own honour, reached a height of 112 feet. It is told that he buried his wife under this main tower and that he lived in constant fear that he might be unable to finish his work himself.

from *Fantastic Architecture*
by Ulrich Conrads and Hans G. Sperlich

What was Sam Rodilla's work: fixing tiles or building towers?

Work is of two kinds: first, altering the position of matter at or near the earth's surface relatively to other such matter; second, telling other people to do so. The first kind is unpleasant and ill paid, the second is pleasant and highly paid.

from *In Praise of Idleness*
by Bertrand Russell

Doing your own thing

At a conference about 'incentives' in industry, the writer Nigel Balchin remarked that: 'Industrial psychologists must stop messing about with tricky and ingenious bonus schemes and find out why a man, after a hard day's work, went home and enjoyed digging in his garden.'

But we can already make a good guess why. He enjoys going home and digging in his garden because there he is free from foremen, managers and bosses. He is free from the slavery of doing the same thing day in day out, and is in control of the whole thing from start to finish. He is free to decide for himself how and when to set about it. He is responsible to himself and not to somebody else. He is working because he *wants* to and not because he *has* to. He is doing his own thing. He is his own man.

If people could pick and choose whether or where to work or not, they would choose to work for themselves. Think of all those people whose secret dream or cherished ambition is to run a small-holding or a little shop or to set up in their own trade on their own account, even though it would mean risking all they had saved, and working night and day. Few of them are optimistic enough to think that they would make a fortune that way: what they want above all is the sense of independence and of controlling their own lives.

Easy enough when a man works on his own, but could it happen when people work in larger numbers? Well, there are a handful of firms in this country controlled by the people who work there. The fishermen of Brixham are an example, and so are the miners of Brora on the coast of Sutherland in Scotland. Ten years ago this pit was to have shut down, but instead the miners took it over after negotiations with the National Coal Board, and formed a company called Highland Colliery Ltd. They are slowly repaying the loan they got from the Highland Fund, and each miner takes up two shares in the company each week. Their output of coal is all used locally and the mine provides a living for the workers and their dependants – about 150 people in all.

Other miners, working for the Coal Board in some of the pits in the Durham coalfield, had the chance of organizing their method of work for themselves in what is known as composite working. All the different jobs involved in mining the coal face were shared out among the miners themselves. The team agreed a price per ton, took on the responsibility and shared the earnings equally.

What is he?

What is he?
– A man, of course.
Yes, but what does he do?
– He lives and is a man.
Oh quite! but he must work. He must have a
  job of some sort.
– Why?
Because obviously he's not one of the
  leisured classes.
– I don't know. He has a lot of leisure. And he
  makes quite beautiful chairs. –
There you are then! He's a cabinet maker.
– No no!
Anyhow a carpenter and joiner.
– Not at all.
But you said so.
– What did I say?
That he made chairs, and was a joiner and
  carpenter.
– I said he made chairs, but I did not
  say he was a carpenter.
All right then, he's just an amateur.
– Perhaps! Would you say that a thrush was
  a professional flautist, or just an amateur? –
I'd say it was just a bird.
– And I say he is just a man.
All right! You always did quibble.

D. H. Lawrence

The Tavistock Institute study of these miners showed 'the ability of quite large primary work groups of forty to fifty members to act as self-regulating, self-developing social organisms able to maintain themselves in a steady state of high productivity'. But could huge factories be run without bosses? You'd have to have a revolution to find out. In Russia, where the revolution was supposed to bring power to the workers, factories are run in the same way as in the West, except that the differences in pay between workers and managers are even greater and the workers can't even go on strike. The one country where industry is officially run by workers' councils is Yugoslavia. Whether you think it really is or not depends on whose propaganda you listen to.

However well or badly the Yugoslav system works, the people there believe in it. A Scottish sociologist was asked quite seriously by a young worker in a factory at Sarajevo, 'Is it true that in England the workers don't manage the factories?'

It *is* true, and this is why we cannot say how workers' control would work. The nearest bit of evidence we can find, to see whether the great pyramid of management is necessary in large-scale modern industry comes from Seymour Melman. He is an American professor of industrial and management engineering and he wanted to compare different ways of organizing the production of a similar object. The example he found was the Ferguson tractor, which at that time was made under licence by Fords in Detroit, USA, and by Standards at Coventry. (This

The shipyard closed but the workers stayed put. Could they run it themselves?

was before Standards sold the tractor factory to the Massey-Ferguson Company, and before Leylands took over Standards.) The system of production operated at the time was the gang system, the tractor factory was organized as one huge gang, and payment was based, not on the output of individual workers, but on that of the whole group. He found, that, contrasted with the American firm, 'thousands of workers operated virtually without supervision as conventionally understood, and at high productivity; the highest wage in British industry was paid; high quality products were produced at acceptable prices in extensively mechanized plants; the management conducted its affairs at unusually low costs; also, organized workers had a substantial role in production decision making.'

All in a day's work 4 ***Serena Wilson, stripper***

'I like the work. It's funny, because everyone asks how I felt when I first danced on stage with no clothes on. It's silly because you're so worried about getting the steps right at the time that you don't think that you're nude at all.

'It may sound corny, but I don't consider myself as a stripper. I started in Paris where the lead dancer in a show is always nude and I sort of progressed from there. At first I was shocked by the idea, but then I got used to it. Now I do a very erotic nude dance with my boy friend Milovan, who I met when we were both at the Folies Bergère.

'At first, I wasn't sure about English audiences because this kind of thing isn't developed and accepted with the same kind of sophistication as it is on the Continent. But now I think people are getting used to more nudity here.

'The money's very good. It has to be good. O.K., so a secretary may not earn even a quarter of what we get. But a secretary can work until she's sixty, whereas we can only go on until thirty-five or so.

'When the body starts to sag, that's it. You're finished. You just hope to have made enough money to start a business of your own – or have enough investments to live off the interest.'

Daily Mirror, 2 July 1971

But suppose the workers took over?

Would they want to go on making the same product in the same way for the same market? Years ago a young French girl, Simone Weil, wanting to find out what work was really like, persuaded a mine-owner to let her go down the pit and find out what it felt like to use a pneumatic drill all day. Then she got a job on the assembly line at the Renault factory. She concluded that it was not enough for the miners to take over the pit and the car workers to take over the factory. They would also have to change the whole technical process to suit the way they *wanted* to work, and would have to ask: Who am I producing this for? Is it worth producing?

Keith Paton recently asked the same questions. Suppose 5000 workers took over the car factory where they had previously been employed. After the carnival of revolution would come the appeals to get back to work. But what sort of work? Who for? And what for?

So instead of restarting the assembly track (if the young workers haven't already smashed it) they spend two months discussing the point of their work, and how to rearrange it. Private cars? Why do people always want to go somewhere else? Is it because where they are is so intolerable? And what part did the car play in making the need to escape? What about day-to-day convenience? Is being stuck in a traffic jam convenient? . . . Have you seen the faces of old people as they try to cross a busy main road? What about the inconvenience to pedestrians? What's the reason for buying a car? Is it just wanting to HAVE it? Do we think the value of a car rubs off on to us? But that's the wrong way round. Does having a car really save time? What's the average hours worked in manufacturing industry? Let's look it up in the library: 45·7 hours work a week. What's the amount of the family's spending money in a week that goes on cars? 10·3 per cent of all family income. Which means more like 20 per cent if you've got a car because half of us don't have one. What's 20 per cent of forty-five hours? Christ, nine hours! That's a hell of a long time spent 'saving time'! There must be a better way of getting from A to B. By bus? OK, let's make buses. But what about all the pollution and that? What about those electric cars they showed on the telly once? And so on.

He thinks that after another month of discussion and research, the workers might decide on splitting up into groups for self-employment in a pattern something like the table shown opposite.

Workers' control debate
You are a worker in that car factory. Put the arguments to your fellow-workers for your choice among the seven working groups. What other groups would you start? Do the others agree? Remember that whatever your group decides it must take account of what is happening in the rest of society. It is no good making monorails if no towns want to install them, or buses if workers in other worker-controlled organizations don't choose to be bus drivers.

Number of workers	*Point*	*Scale of use*	*Scale of making*	*Technical mode*
185	*Car refurbishing* (to increase use-value of models already on the road, e.g. by adding exhaust filters).	Community.	Small community factory.	Varied – little end-product specialization due to variety of makes and problems.
1850	Buses, for connecting train and monorail termini with where people want to go.	National (also part regional, part export and part give-away – voluntary overseas aid).	Large regional factory, plus several smaller parts factories in communities in the region. (Also, not included in the 1850, parts from outside the region.)	Regional factory not on shift work or automatic track. Gangs of men who see whole buses through to completion, including distribution. Smaller parts factories make standardized parts, therefore high level of automation.
740	Overhead monorail cars.	Regional (and small surplus exchanged with other regions), i.e. on a national basis.	Small regional factory, smaller parts factories.	As above except only quasi-automatic machinery (e.g. Leaver and Brown drilling machine).
555	Electric cars and scooters for disabled people and inner city travel especially.	Regional.	Two small community factories of 250, making the engines. Glass fibre and plastics factory for bodywork.	Glass fibre and plastics factory at high level of automation.
370	White bicycles for communal use.	Community.	Neighbourhood workshops for kit construction and frame manufacture – parts from community factories, regional factories.	Automation for ball bearings, hubs, in community factories. Regionally produced standard steel tubing. Made into bicycles by neighbourhood craft work and kit construction.
925	Construction of dignified housing with built-in communal potential, communal centres and workshops.	Task forces attached to neighbourhoods.	Great variety of work – some construction standardization with prefabricated modules, but no standardization of design.	
375	Dropouts from organized work – some do minimal work (say five hours gardening a week). 15 per cent dropout ration at first, reduces to $7\frac{1}{2}$ per cent as many drift into congenial milieux. This $7\frac{1}{2}$ per cent largely compensated for by the number of casual *drop-in* workers at community and neighbourhood levels, especially in communal construction work. Kids and old people like to make themselves useful. Important to create a reasonable subsistence existence for non-workers, otherwise theft, antagonisms, stigma, etc. Antagonisms diminish when people enjoy their own work, and therefore don't resent 'skivers'. Diminished fear of not-working leads to more rational attitude to the point of work: OK to take plenty of breaks, etc.			

from *Work and Surplus* by Keith Paton

Face to face with ourselves

He paced about a little and began again, 'You are like all our magistrates, who condemn men to prisons they themselves have never lived in, like company directors who haven't the slightest idea of what it is like to work on a production line, like old ladies shovelling coal on to their fires without the faintest glimmer of what it is like to go down a mine and dig out the coal. You are all each other's gaolers. You keep a dustbin and then condemn a man to whom you are a complete stranger to spend his days coping with your dirt and refuse. Goodness knows he hates the job, who wouldn't, so you have to say to him, as they do in gaols, that if he doesn't do as you wish you will give him nothing but bread and water.' 'He should get a better job,' I said, crossing my legs the other way. 'There are plenty about.' 'But somebody must empty your dustbin, Mr Smallcreep. If not him then someone else, or no doubt there would be a great commotion with you at its centre. Likewise, when you buy food you oblige a man to go out into the fields to grow it for you. Buy any manufactured article and you condemn, or, if you like, blackmail or bribe, a man to spend his waking hours in a factory. All these people in their turn will condemn you to waste your life perhaps in some office or at some other machine, doing for them what you have prevented them from doing for themselves. In a free society, however, you would have no such claims over complete strangers. They would help you if they felt like it, if you were a particularly generous-natured or endearing person. But if you were not then you would have to empty your own dustbin, and dispose of your own sewage, and cure your own sickness. In a free society you would have to come to terms with yourself and with others like yourself, with the man who backs his car into yours, with the man next door who has to feed three times as many mouths as you do, with the drunks who get into your garden. You would have to sort things out with them yourself, instead of having social workers or political parties or policemen or shop stewards to do the job for you, and in the process you would be forced to face up to what sort of person you yourself really were.'

from *Smallcreep's Day* by Peter Brown

On the moon an astronaut is a completely independent, self-contained man. Like the Eskimo on page 5 he has to be. Yet in another way he is the most completely controlled worker there has ever been. Even his sleep is managed by Ground Control. Have astronauts come face to face with themselves? Is sweeping up moondust a man's job?